AMANDA FE

CW00740000

SONGS

OF

heaven

WRITING SONGS FOR
CONTEMPORARY WORSHIP

SECOND EDITION

First published by SHOUT! Publishing
PO Box 1195, Castle Hill NSW 1765, Australia
shoutpublishing.com

Scripture taken from the HOLY BIBLE, NEW INTERNATIONAL VERSION®
Copyright© 1973, 1978, 1984 by International Bible Society. Used by permission of Zondervan Publishing House. All rights reserved.

The "NIV" and "New International Version" trademarks are registered in the United States Patent and Trademark Office by International Bible Society. Use of either trademark requires the permission of International Bible Society.

Scripture taken from THE MESSAGE. Copyright© 1993, 1994, 1995, 1996, 2000, 2001, 2002. Used by permission of NavPress Publishing Group.

All comments from Hillsong songwriters have been quoted with their permission. The writers include Darlene Zschech, Joel Houston, Marty Sampson, Mia Fielder, Tanya Riches, Reuben Morgan, Raymond Badham, Jonathon Douglass, and Miriam Webster, Ben Fielding, Ben Hastings and Brooke Ligertwood, Hannah Hobbs, Matt Crocker

All quotations from Hillsong songs used with permission.

For full reference to Hillsong songs used in this book, please see page 319

ISBN: 978-1-922076-62-5

CONTENTS

INTRODUCTORY THOUGHTS

'The church that I see is a worshipping church whose songs reflect such a passion for Christ that others sense His magnificence and power. A distinct sound that emanates from a healthy church, contagious in spirit – creating music that resounds from villages and tribes to great cities and nations.'[1]

Brian Houston – The church that I now see

'Praise the Lord. Sing to the Lord a new song, his praise in the assembly of his faithful people.' (Psalm 149:1 NIV)

'When people enter these doors – the literal House of God, the Gateway to Heaven – they should hear something that sounds different from what they know. It is more than lyrics and melodies, they are songs from Heaven that carry the breath of God to dry and thirsty hearts. I love our church because those gifted and anointed to lead in his arena have devoted themselves to 'their secret place with their King,' and they return to us with songs from another world. They bring a taste of Heaven to earth that refreshes and ignites the hearts of humanity. Their songs gives us a beautiful vehicle upon which to express our love to God...and the whole experience of unrestrained, extravagant worship is captivating beyond expression....'[2]

Bobbie Houston

---

1   Brian Houston *The Church that I now see* 2014
2   Bobbie Houston *Heaven is in this House* Maximised Leadership Inc. Australia 2001 p. 151

'Instead be filled with the Spirit, speaking to one another with psalms, hymns and songs from the Spirit. Sing and make music from your heart to the Lord...' (Ephesians 5:18, 19 NIV)

FOREWORD
TO THE 2ND EDITION
WORDS AND MUSIC:

12 notes of infinite wonder by Joel Houston

The art of writing a song is as simple as it is impossible. In the same way faith is. It's all grace.

An invitation to participate in something altogether other-worldly, by way of simply having breath. You or I don't earn our breath, any more than the voice that sings the song we're given to sing. Our faith is exhibited in the grace to respond—and ultimately, that is all our songs are—a response. An exhale put to words and music given in return for every inhale received. We've been singing since our first infant-cry in response to life. If you can accept this simple truth, you're ready to write songs, because the way I see it, song writing is simply putting words and music to the gift of breath, as a means to saying thank you.

I found God when the song found me.

As a child who wanted to be anywhere but behind a piano, I despised the construct-torture of forced musical learning. And though my parents assured me one day I'd be grateful they paid their good money to give me piano lessons I considered the thirty minutes staring malevolently at the ebony and ivory laid out before me the bane of my adolescent existence. I couldn't imagine then how wrong I was, and right my parents would be.

But music changed, the moment my piano teacher changed tact. Perhaps my lack of passion was becoming clear in my lack of performance. The progress of my form and technique a stunted snail pace. Finger stuttering scales, and clunky accidental jazz recitals of green leaves and Richard Marx. The day came, where at the end of our lesson he simply said "you have one task this week.... to write a song". My ears immediately swung open, "what do you mean?.. out of nothing?" "Yeah, just play whatever you hear, and if you hear nothing, just play notes until you do."

I couldn't wait to get home and give it a go. I ran straight to the old piano in the study, and stared down at the same 88 notes I long despised, and saw a whole new world opening up at my fingertips. The black and whites suddenly busting with a sense of living colour. I counted the notes, twelve of them, between middle C and B, holding every melody ever written, and an infinite well of future possibilities to find. Like twelve hours of morning, twelve hours of evening, twelve months in a year, twelve tribes, twelve disciples—as if to remind us that within a limited number of ordinary notes, or ordinary people, or in the limitations of a day, a night, a year—God can do infinite things. I held an octave with my left hand, and played a scale, Doe-ray-me-far-so-la-tee-doe, seven notes of creation, the eighth the same as the first, like eternity, the end a new beginning, new creation, the Kingdom. I played a chord, a simple first, third and fifth. Three-in-one. Like the trinity in perfect harmony. I discovered the beauty in tension and release, the minor fall, and the major lift—like God is always redemptive. I found beauty in dissidence, in conflict and resolution, light and shade, the beauty of negative space. The way melody can move in harmony, with more effectiveness than it can in and of itself—like two becoming one, and creating a third more beautiful sound. And it all works in rhythm, and time and pitch. I discovered God in the music, and in the music I discovered how God is an artist. He doesn't hold us to the religious bounds of form and technique. The rudimentary obedience of rules, obliging the construct patterns of the past. God doesn't want a church to simply follow the crotchet and quaver patterns of yesterday's songs—much like His Word, spoken in light, and life and love—it is more than mere ink binding us to a static absolute truth. God is always moving, breathing, creating, redeeming, restoring, revising and revealing His work, in and through us, like Words and music. He wants our songs, much like our lives and our churches, to be as abounding in flesh and blood as we are Spirit. To imitate, reflect, and ultimately become the embodiment of His spirit, His life, His light and His life—like Jesus, Word made Flesh. And it's all grace. That's the honest God to truth.

Our songs should sing like our lives do. Not just within the walls of our churches, and homes—but wherever there are people. Wherever there is pain, suffering, hurt and heart break. Wherever there are questions, confusion, chaos and disorder—wherever there is an opportunity to bring light, and life and love into the atmosphere, may we find the words and music to do so.

Let the melody run, may it find harmony with others, may we altogether find our place within the rhythm and heartbeat of the God who holds all things together, and aligns all our dissident parts, within the pitch-shift wonder of His grace, and if you have a voice, breath in your lungs, and a heart beating in your chest, then let it sing the exhale praises it was made to. Ever in response, ever in reflection, ever in new revelations of the love than runs through life and death, and in and through you and me, everyone and everything, with the sound of a new song, as timeless as the old ones, vintage as the heavens, new as the morning, the future, the kingdom, and all its infinite possibilities.

Songs are always, in some way collaborative. Be it writing with others, or words inspired by someone else's words—conversations, teaching, something borrowed, something learned, something you heard. Rhythms and melodies that moved you at one time or another, or caused you to feel something you never had. Our songs are always in some way, and extension of the sum of its parts, and more than anything, the sum of the parts attributed the credit.

No more is that true, than for Amanda, (and her husband Robert), affectionately I call them A&R which in the "music biz", would otherwise be acronymic for "Artist Relations"—the talent finder, and more often the ego-inflater mending the relationship between artist and label. In this sense, A&R (Amanda and Robert) embody an antithetical spin on Artist Relations, in so much that relationally, they have helped shape and frame the Art and Artists of our church, with kind-assassination of the kind of egos too often synonymous with those who attach their heart too closely to their talent. In this sense, A&R have relentlessly served the body of songs flowing from our little church to the world for the longest time—often anonymously, thanklessly, and with patient-long-suffering usually reserved for a spoiled kid's mother and father. And that they have become. Graciously giving their time to help frame the theology of our art, our songs, and in so doing—helped to frame and inspire the theology of our hearts. A&R became a necessary abbreviation, so frequent are our emails in the heat of a project. Some of our email chains have been the most enjoyable of conversations, (I must emphasise 'most'), because I'm sure Amanda would agree, there have been plenty that fall a little shy in the moment of immediate joy—but such is the process—and it's one I have been forever grateful for.

Over many years, Amanda has cast her heart and mind into the negative space behind and in-between every word you see printed on our Hillsong lyric sheets. Often helping our writers see things they haven't seen, understand complexities of thought and emotional conflicts of poetry and theology, and pushing many a song from ok, to something richer.

There are few I could imagine more qualified to write, as beautifully as she does, on behalf of these songs amongst the wealth of songs past, present and future, with particular intention given the highest call for any song—to give our theology a voice, and our soul something to sing to the God it belongs to.

There is a cosmic need for divine thought on how to keep pushing the limits, and holding true to the necessary margins, in pursuit of an infinite song. It's a constant challenge to be using art, with the responsibility of theology, accessibility, and inclusivity. It's a fine line at times, a death wobbles balancing act at others. It requires obedience and rebellion, dissatisfaction and submission, courage and humility, willingness and reluctance, ability and inadequacy, passion and surrender, prophecy and orthodoxy, spirit and flesh, truth and grace, and grace upon grace after that.

Amanda understands the tension and release, the conflict and resolution, and the wonder of words and music, to change the world.

The best songs are the ones that tell the truth, And the truth is grace. So you have everything you need to not just sing it, like you breath—but to write it, and let it breathe inside-out, in and through someone like you, because it's always been this way—for all our limitation, Infinite wonder abound, and they have a sound. Can you hear it?

If you can't, just start playing, singing, writing. Start by letting go. It's the best way to find something new.

And if none of that helps, the ensuing pages are a wealth of better wisdom, certain to inspire, challenge and practically help you.

......and lastly, let me take this page space, at this moment to publicly say on behalf of all the writers who been so fortunate,

Thank you Amanda.

We love you.

FOREWORD TO THE 1ST EDITION
by Darlene Zschech

There are many thousands of highly gifted people across the earth who are designed to give voice, through music and prose, melody and song, to the adoration and prayers of ordinary men, women and children to our Lord and King. This God song, a song born through revelation and often through much 'life' , has been spoken about so often, but never have I heard this mystery of songs in worship explained so brilliantly as when I first heard Amanda speak on this subject.

I have hounded her for a long time to get this teaching out in book form, as I truly believe it to be revolutionary in unveiling understanding to those entrusted with this amazing responsibility.

The very first time I wrote a song that was sung by my local church, was when I was newly saved, at fifteen years old…and to be honest, rather than feeling elated at the opportunity, I was quite overwhelmed at the level of responsibility of putting words to our Saviour, in someone else's mouth! From that moment, and for next few years, I concentrated on writing sloppy love songs instead and steered clear from the spiritual weight I was sensing when it came to writing songs of worship and praise.

Ever so gently, over seasons and time, surrounded by some beautiful men and woman of God who graciously and patiently showed me how to live this life under Christ. the songs started to come again. This time however, as my heart was prepared with greater knowledge and my soul was no longer satisfied with music for music's sake, confidence began to arise in me, that just maybe I could play a part in this song gathering momentum across the ages and throughout history, defying denominational barriers and preferences…

It makes me smile to this day, that yes, the musical craftsmen and lyrical scribes have always been needed to take their place when it comes to arresting the senses of humanity…but there is also a place for those like me, who have limited knowledge but who are filled with a unrelenting passion to do all they can possibly do to bring the sound of heaven to earth, and unleash the songs for the ordinary man and woman as you'll notice that often the songs that become the modern day hymns and anthems of our time, are quite uncomplicated. But rather, give voice to the heart, the prayers and cries of everyday people. Aah, there is nothing quite like the sound of the church in song, the church, the body, coming together and laying aside their own desires and even tastes, to give voice to the heavenly song of worship and praise, raising up a standard,…where history and eternity meet.

I pray that as you begin to read, you will be inspired and challenged, to approach this gift with a far greater dimension of thoughtfulness AND confidence that what you bring to the table matters.

Your songs may only ever be for the ultimate audience of ONE but don't be too discouraged and frustrated, for to be honest, I would much rather be found there any day, on my knees, in Truth and Sincerity, delighting the heart of my Lord and King than trying to write to please the heart and ears of man.

Read on, and may inspiration and peace be yours, for now and evermore.

With much love, Darlene. (2005)

WHY I WANTED
TO WRITE THIS BOOK

I have always loved singing. At school I joined choirs, madrigal groups and vocal ensembles of various types and especially loved singing all the traditional carols at Christmas even though I was not a Christian at that point. During my High School years I had the privilege of training as a classical musician at Trinity College, London, and spent every Saturday there. Part of that training was in composition and I had to produce a piece of music every week, some of which I must confess I wrote just before class on the train going up to London! Life was filled with music of all types. I was a child of the 60s and 70s and so taught myself to play the guitar and to sing songs by Joan Baez and Bob Dylan while also singing Bach and Mozart at college.

Then at the end of 1971, in a little Anglican church in Surrey, England, I became a Christian and my life changed for ever. In 1972 I sensed that God was calling me into the ministry and in 1973 I began to study for a degree in Theology at Nottingham University and joined the Christian Union. There, for the first time, I heard contemporary worship choruses and immediately loved them. Here was a way to express my new found love for God in simple yet profound words and in music which did not require any vocal training to be able to sing them. Not all the choruses were equally inspiring but many have stayed in my spirit all these years later. My husband, Robert, ministered out of a church in Nottingham and I became involved in the worship team there and began to write a few worship songs for the church.

When we moved to Sydney in 1990 I taught song writing for many years in what is now Hillsong College although these days my focus is more on teaching theological subjects. For a long time I had wanted to convey some of what I had both taught to and learned from my songwriting students and in 2004 in conversations with Darlene Zschech, who was at that time our Worship Pastor, I discovered that it was also on her heart to pass on what we have learned on our journey. This book is an attempt to do just that. It is by no means an exhaustive work on song writing and I realise that there are many excellent resources in the marketplace already but, hopefully, it will serve as another helpful tool for those who want to develop their skills.

This completely revised edition takes into account the journey that we have been on as a church over the twelve years since the book was published and draws on fresh insight and wisdom from our songwriters. My own role has also developed and changed as regards songwriting as my husband Robert and I have been responsible over the past ten years or so for checking the lyrics of every song that comes out of the church. I will say more about that exciting, creative and challenging journey later!

I have not written this book primarily as a songwriter but as a teacher. My desire has always been that my students will learn things from me that will enable them to far surpass anything I could ever write. This means that I am not interested in turning out clones who will only produce exactly what I would write or choose to listen to but I want to teach principles of song writing that will equip individuals to express themselves in their own unique, God-given way. I have watched my students over the years develop as songwriters and produce worship songs for their home churches and that brings more satisfaction than almost anything else. I treasure the worship albums they send me, often from other nations.

I have also watched our own songwriters at Hillsong church develop in their gifts and hopefully have been a small part of some of their journeys as we have discussed, disagreed at times, but always sought to bring out the best in their songs.

So, why have I written this book?

Because I believe that worship is a vital part of our existence

I am totally convinced that worship is fundamental to our existence as Christians and that to worship God in spirit and truth is one of the most important things we can do. I am convinced that words and music together have great power to move and inspire the human heart. I remember, before I became a Christian, singing in a performance of Bach's St. Matthew's Passion with tears pouring down my face at the combination of the beauty of the soaring melodies and rich harmonies with the story of Jesus' last hours. Perhaps that sounds like emotion rather than a spiritual experience but I know that it had a lasting impact and that, years later, listening to St. Matthew's Passion still has the power to draw me into worship and wonder at the love of Jesus.

The songs that we sing to express our worship are very powerful because they can either help or hinder that process. I have sung songs, often very simple songs, that seem to have so much the touch of heaven on them that I found myself caught up in adoration. I have also sung songs that have had the opposite result as I have struggled with dubious theology, uninspired melodies and lack of focus.

Because I am passionate about communicating truth

As a teacher of biblical theology as well as of music, I am passionate about truth. When words are set to music they tend to stick in the mind. Songs were one of the great teaching tools down the centuries before the Bible was readily available to all and before literacy was widespread. Great truths would be set to music and would back up the priest's sermons. Sadly many of the choruses and hymns we sing today have not had careful attention paid to the biblical validity of their lyrics which, at best, reduces their effectiveness and, at worst, can lead to error. This is something that I feel passionately about and will tackle in this book.

Because I want to encourage a new generation of songwriters

God has graciously favoured the songs we have been writing at Hillsong church over the past few years and, hopefully, that has inspired others to try writing their own songs. At Hillsong church our desire has always been to serve the body of Christ and so it seemed to be a good idea to share some of the lessons and principles that we have learned. To this end I have included numerous references to Hillsong materials and reflections from a number of our songwriters. None of us would claim to be experts. We are just a group of people who love God and who are having a go, but along the way we have learned a few things and maybe they will help you in your journey.

In this book we are looking at a specific type of worship song that could loosely be defined as contemporary worship and I am very aware that there is so much other wonderful music in existence. However much of it, while it has the breath of God on it, speaks in the musical language of a different age. Our passion at Hillsong is that the church will easily be able to relate to the songs we sing. However we do try to include a diversity of expression in our services from time to time. Increasingly as our church has become more global in its campuses and reach we are aware of the variety of expressions of worship. And we love to draw from the riches that are both around us now and from the past as is apparent perhaps in more recent settings of old hymns such as 'Cornerstone' and 'Amazing Grace'.

A GUIDE TO USING THIS BOOK

This book follows a fairly simple pattern. Each chapter contains some basic principles and tips along with a summary and practical exercises to try. I have also included examples, wherever possible, of songs that illustrate what I am teaching and excerpts throughout the book from out songwriters talking about specific songs and themes. Most of these examples I have drawn from Hillsong material but occasionally I have referred to other songs as well. I have included details of all the songs mentioned in Appendix C.

The songs I have chosen are simply examples to illustrate a point. They are certainly not the only ones I could have chosen or even necessarily the best ones but I have tried to choose songs that are readily available either from our recent resources or that are widely known. In revising the book I have needed to remove some of the examples from the older songs in order to make room for the many new songs and also some of the original comments from songwriters to allow for a greater range of voices. This is not to say that either the comments or the song examples were any less valid but it is simply an attempt to draw on more recent material.

This book is not intended as an exhaustive text on song writing but rather as a starting point. It is deliberately narrow in its focus on writing for worship although most of the principles can equally well be applied to other songs that you might write.

If you are a complete beginner I suggest that you start at the beginning and work your way through. This book is not intended as a guide to music theory so you will need to supplement it with relevant material if your musical skills are limited. For more experienced songwriters there will still hopefully be useful information and interesting exercises that will stretch you.

One way to work could be to find other songwriters in your local area who would be interested in studying the book with you. You could set up your own songwriting workshop and gain the benefits of other people's input into your songs. It is also a great way to find other writers with whom you may be able to co-write songs.

There is no substitute for simply having a go. I have talked to enough good songwriters to know that the best way to learn to write songs is actually to write songs. It is no good reading this book or other books on song writing and thinking that you are now a songwriter. You have to write songs and you may write twenty songs before you write one that you think is any good, but none of those twenty is wasted because they have all contributed to the twenty first. So read on and start writing!

Joel Houston on the album Zion

'This is why we undertook this project in the first place; not to just add another worship title to the catalogue, or to fulfill the project quota!! The opposite, we did it because we believe that God is wild enough to entrust us with His song and His message, and use us to display it the best we can to others.' Joel Houston on the reasons behind the album 'Zion'[3] *– 27.2.13*

---

3 Joel Houston - 'Joel Houston talks ZION' https://hillsong.com/collected/blog/2013/02/joel-houston-talkszion/#. WVSjuliGOM8 7/2/2013 Used by permission

REFLECTING ON WORSHIP

'Sing God a brand-new song!
Earth and everyone in it, sing!
Sing to God—worship God!' (PSALM 96:1 THE MESSAGE)

'Songwriters in our community are the poets and prophets. Their words and melodies create beauty and cause the church to see who God is and what He is like. They help us to hear what God imagines for us and our future. By painting a reality that we endeavour to live, songs give us anthems to congregate around as a community, but also something that reverberates into our homes and daily lives. They mark significant milestones like births, deaths and marriages and are like modern day Psalms being sung as we journey towards God. Good songs make the scriptures come alive and ground our faith and understanding. They give us insight and wisdom for our everyday reality and are vehicles for navigating the good and the bad times.

Songs paint pictures and give expression to the deepest longing in our heart. Often you can almost hear the people gasp in wonder when a song is presented for the first time and they find themselves caught up in new ways of expressing what they know to be true. New songs keep faith alive and vibrant and fresh. It's like turning the light on and seeing again what has always been right in front of you. Our song writers are a gift to the people of God as they create vocabulary that deepens and heightens the way we talk about Jesus, Gods great salvation plans and the Holy spirits enduring presence and empowerment.'

Cassandra Langton

'When you write songs that people sing as part of their worship to God, there is a bit of your soul that shares the aches of those around you. When there is tragedy, the song of lament wakes up with you, and when there is joy, the sound of praise fills your ears. To some it might seem odd to reach for a guitar when tears are falling on scuffed up shoes, but I really don't know any other way of being.'[4]

Reuben Morgan

4 Reuben Morgan – 'Return to the Cornerstone' https://hillsong.com/collected/blog/2012/06/return-to-the-cornerstone/#. WVSRHIiGOM8 12/6/2012 Used by permission.

CHAPTER 1

A THEOLOGY
OF WORSHIP

by Robert Fergusson

I n the Christian community, the word 'worship' is used in such a variety of ways that its meaning has become clouded. For instance, some say, "We come together to 'worship' on a Sunday morning". For these people, worship describes our corporate expression and adoration of God. Whereas, others say, "We sing songs of praise and then we start to 'worship'". In this case, it seems the concept of 'worship' has been reduced to the quieter songs at the end of a song list. But is this the way the Bible defines worship?

Certain things defy definition. A kiss is one example. Worship is another. In both cases, a dictionary definition falls hopelessly short. We may be able to explain the mechanics, but how can we possibly describe the mystery? Yet at the beginning of a book on writing songs for worship that is exactly what we have to do. Unless we attempt to express what the Bible says about worship, this book will only strengthen the hands of songwriters, without inspiring the hearts of worshippers. Worshippers sing songs from a converted soul - their songs are birthed in transformation. So what is worship? What exactly is this word which causes creation to sing?

How does the Bible describe worship?

There are numerous references and descriptions of worship in the Bible. The first of which is found in the shocking account of Abraham offering his son Isaac to God. Abraham says to his servant, "Stay here with the donkey while I and the boy go over there. We will *worship* and then we will come back to you" (Genesis 22:5) (Italics mine). There is no mention here of music. No gathered congregation. No songs. It is a story of single-minded obedience, a sacrifice, and the intervention of God. The word used in the Hebrew (Heb. Shachah) means to "bow down" or to "prostrate oneself"5 in an act of reverence. So is worship an act of sacrifice to God?

In the New Testament, two Greek words are commonly used for worship. The writer to the Hebrews uses the word 'latreuo' when he challenges them to "worship God acceptably with reverence and awe" (Hebrews 12:28). This word can be translated worship or serve. The Lord Jesus Christ uses the Greek word 'proskuneo' when he says, "a time is coming and has now come when the true worshippers will worship the Father in spirit and truth, for they are the kind of worshippers the Father seeks" (John 4:23). The word 'proskuneo' means, "To kiss the hand to (towards) one, in token of reverence"6. Once again, there is no mention here of music, songs or song-writing. Although, as we shall see, songs can be a powerful expression of our worship and also can enable us to worship more effectively, worship is evidently far more fundamental.

---

5   *Enhanced Strong's Lexicon*, Oak Harbor, WA: Logos Research Systems, Inc. 1995.
6   *Enhanced Strong's Lexicon*, Oak Harbor, WA: Logos Research Systems, Inc. 1995.

In all of these, and other Biblical examples, worship is seen to be a reverential attitude of someone or something toward the One from whom they came. Angels worship the God who commands them (Hebrews 1:6); creation reveres its Creator (Psalm 148) and humanity glorifies its Maker (Psalm 95:6). This attitude of reverence is usually expressed in an act of service. True worship, it seems, has more to do with a reverential attitude and an act of service than it does to a song. Further, the English word 'worship' is rooted in the word 'worth'. Worship, therefore, is about an acknowledgement of worth; a recognition and response of honour to someone who is worthy. This is the heart and lifestyle from which a song of worship is sung.

Worship is the necessary response of the created for the Creator

The concept of worship is inbuilt into the heart of every human being. It seems, we need to give glory to someone or something. If we don't worship God, we find ourselves worshipping someone or something else. If we don't have a god, we will make one (Isaiah 44:15-17; Acts 17:23). The object of our worship is determined by our belief system. If we believe we are self-made, we will tend to give glory to ourselves and honour our own achievements; we will applaud our own creativity. If, on the other hand, we believe we are the product of nature, our tendency is to exalt the world in which we live. We will elevate animals above humanity, we'll seek guidance in the stars and worship the heavens (Acts 7:42). As Paul the apostle put it, we worship the created rather the Creator.

> For since the creation of the world God's invisible qualities—
> his eternal power and divine nature—have been clearly seen,
> being understood from what has been made, so that men are
> without excuse. For although they knew God, they neither

glorified him as God nor gave thanks to him, but their thinking became futile and their foolish hearts were darkened. Although they claimed to be wise, they became fools and exchanged the glory of the immortal God for images made to look like mortal man and birds and animals and reptiles. Therefore God gave them over in the sinful desires of their hearts to sexual impurity for the degrading of their bodies with one another. They exchanged the truth of God for a lie, and worshiped and served created things rather than the Creator— who is forever praised. Amen. (ROMANS 1:20-25)

If, however, we believe that God created us, He becomes the object of our affection and reverence. He is the One we choose to serve. In simplistic terms, these then are the three choices we have: We can serve ourselves; we can serve the earth; or we can serve the God who made them both. In other words, we can worship our own creativity (which includes our gifts or talents), the created (which includes anything which is created as well as ourselves), or the Creator Himself. The object of our worship is the battle ground of the soul. When Satan, a created being, challenged Jesus in the wilderness, he wanted the Christ to worship him. When presented with the same challenge, our response should be the same as Jesus': "Worship the Lord your God and serve him only" (Matthew 4:10). This choice is the foundation for our fulfilment and success.

The Bible makes it very clear that God created human beings in His image and chose us specifically to give Him praise.

"But you are a chosen people, a royal priesthood, a holy nation, a people belonging to God, that you may declare the praises of him who called you out of darkness into his wonderful light". (1 PETER 2:9)

Like a violin in the hands of its maker, we are created to make an ordered and beautiful sound for the use and pleasure of our Creator. Like a pot in the hands of a potter, we are created to say something of worth about our Creator and do something of value for Him. Our correct response sees our created purpose fulfilled. It is only as we learn to worship God that we discover our God-given destiny. Worship, then, is the necessary and vital response of the created for the Creator.

Worship involves both awe and adoration

The coming of the Lord Jesus Christ has enabled us to approach God with confidence (Hebrews 4:16), but how do we respond appropriately to One whom Jesus Himself described both as a Loving Father (John 16:27) and also One to be feared (Luke 12:5)? It seems that there needs be a combined adoration and awe in our approach. On the one hand, we are drawn by compassion and acceptance to worship with gratitude and freedom, and yet, on the other hand, we, "worship God acceptably with reverence and awe, for our 'God is a consuming fire'" (Hebrews 12:29). There is clearly a necessary tension in worship. Not a negative tension but a positive one – the tension of a violin string – a balance of extremes.

This tension is found in many aspects of worship. For instance, Jesus Christ desires us to worship both in spirit and in truth (John 4:23). Similarly, when Paul the apostle encouraged the churches in Colosse and Ephesus to sing spiritual songs, he taught them to be filled with both the word and the Spirit.

> *"Let the word of Christ dwell in you richly as you teach and admonish one another with all wisdom, and as you sing psalms, hymns and spiritual songs with gratitude in your hearts to God".* (COLOSSIANS 3:16)

*"Do not get drunk on wine, which leads to debauchery.
Instead, be filled with the Spirit. Speak to one another with
psalms, hymns and spiritual songs. Sing and make music
in your heart to the Lord, always giving thanks to God the
Father for everything, in the name of our Lord Jesus Christ".*
(EPHESIANS 5:18-20)

Clearly, some aspects of worship can be defined, explained and taught but there are other aspects which are beyond understanding and defy description. True worship involves both priest and prophet, the predictable and the unpredictable, the expected and the unexpected, the rejected and the respectable. Worship, like music, is both a science and an art. When the composer and conductor Leonard Bernstein attempted to describe music he writes that it is an "utterly satisfying combination of mathematics and magic"[7] The only way to describe it is to be immersed. The same is true of worship. The only way to understand it is to worship God and then the songs we sing will reflect the balance of awe and adoration that comes from our immersion into Christ.

7   Leonard Bernstein. *The Joy of Music*. Panther Books USA 1969.

CHAPTER 2

THE POWER OF A
SONG SUNG TO GOD

My husband, Robert, says that one of the saddest verses in the Bible is to be found in Exodus 32:18. Moses had been on Mount Sinai for forty days receiving direction from God for His covenant people. Meanwhile these same covenant people waiting at the bottom of the mountain had become impatient and fearful and so they persuaded Aaron to make a golden calf for them to worship. As Moses descended the mountain, sounds from the camp reached him. Joshua, who was with him, thought that the camp must have been attacked but Moses knew better: 'It is not the sound of victory, it is not the sound of defeat; it is the sound of singing that I hear.'(Exodus 32:18 NIV)

What they were hearing was the sound of the Israelites worshipping an idol that could do nothing for them and forgetting the God who had brought them out of Egypt with powerful acts of deliverance (Psalm 106:13) It seems amazing that the people could so quickly forget what God had done for them just because Moses had been gone for a while but that is what happened and it's a warning to us. Their songs were empty and powerless, achieving nothing except to rouse God's anger against them. This was a tragic example of a song that was powerless because it was directed to the wrong person. Our songs of worship must be sung to God if they are to be powerful songs

There are times however when even songs that are directed to God can lack power. Jesus addressed this when he spoke to the Pharisees about the hypocrisy of lives that did not match up to their worship:

'These people honour me with their lips; but their hearts are far from me. They worship me in vain; their teachings are but rules taught by men.' (Mark 7:6,7 NIV)

He taught that powerful worship is inseparably connected to spirit and truth. Our worship must be based in reality and come out of the depths of who we are. We cannot worship powerfully and effectively if our hearts are cold or our minds are elsewhere.

I like the way the Message Bible puts it: 'It's who you are and the way you live that count before God. Your worship must engage your spirit in the pursuit of truth. That's the kind of people the Father is out looking for: those who are simply and honestly themselves before him in their worship. God is sheer being itself – Spirit. Those who worship him must do it out of their very being, their spirits, their true selves, in adoration." (John 4:23,24 – The Message)

This chapter is not a theology of song. It is really a series of anecdotes, images and reflections on songs that, when sung out of the heart to God, can carry great power. Songs in themselves are simply songs but the faith attached to them and the truth contained in their words is what makes them powerful. In their different ways all the categories of song described in this chapter are songs of faith and all are found in the Bible. In Appendix A at the end of the book I look at the different themes in the Psalms that relate to the themes described below.

A song of wonder

'Praise the Lord.
Praise the Lord, O my soul.
I will praise the Lord all my life;
I will sing praise to my God as long as I live"

(PSALM 146:1,2 NIV)

C.S. Lewis described praise as 'inner health made audible'[8] and this seems to me to sum up the power of praise. If we are finding it hard to praise God for who He is and what He has done then it is time to take a look at the state of our hearts. Our natural instinct when considering the amazing God who has created us, saved us and cares for us minute by minute should be one of praise. And as we share that wonder and delight in our God with others our own faith and love is renewed.

Sometimes we can find that we are writing a lot of testimony songs in which we thank God for specific things that He has done but we lose that pure focus on praising God for who He is. These songs of wonder, more than almost any others, raise our eyes from our little worlds and preoccupations to see the bigness of our God. Many of the expressions of worship in Revelation fit into this category (Revelation 4:8, 11; 4:12,13). These songs allow us to share our enjoyment of God in corporate worship.

A song of victory

'Then Moses and the Israelites sang this song to the Lord:
'I will sing to the Lord,
For he is highly exalted

---

8   C.S. Lewis *Reflections on the Psalms* from Selected Books Harper Collins UK 1999 p.694

The horse and its rider
He has hurled into the sea.'
(EXODUS 15:1 NIV)

———

This was the most famous victory in the Old Testament as the people celebrated their deliverance from Egypt but, in the New Testament, we find a hymn celebrating the most powerful and famous victory of all:

———

'Therefore God exalted him to the highest place
And gave him the name that is above every name;
That at the name of Jesus every knee should bow,
In heaven and on earth and under the earth;
And every tongue confess that Jesus Christ is Lord.
To the glory of God the Father.'
(PHILIPPIANS 2:9,10 NIV)

———

There is a place in our worship for songs that celebrate the victory that we have in Christ and again these are songs of faith that build our faith as we sing them. It is noteworthy that these songs are often sung before we experience the victory in our own lives just as Jehoshaphat sang a victory song as he marched out into battle (2 Chronicles 20:21,22) rather than waiting until after the victory was won. It was while they sang that God acted on their behalf. It reminds me of a prophecy in Isaiah 30:27-33 that speaks of the same thing. The people were told to sing as on a night of festival while the Lord defeated their enemies. Our faith expressed in a victory song has power as David expressed in Psalm 8.

———

'From the lips of children and infants
You have ordained praise

Because of your enemies,
To silence the foe and the avenger.'
(PSALM 8: 2 NIV)

———

I have many testimonies to this in my own life but I'd like to share just one where singing a song containing words of truth brought victory. It was a sunny afternoon in the late summer of 1987 and I was cooking sate chicken. I put on my oven gloves to adjust the pan and then threw them over my shoulder as I always did when they were not in use. I carried on cooking and it was not until I felt a searing pain on my back and smelt smoke that I became aware that something was wrong. Without realising it I had caught the edge of the gloves on the gas flame and that flame had now burnt through both my shirt and singlet and was burning my flesh. Panicking, I ran out of the kitchen into the living room and into a draught. Immediately the flames seized on the additional oxygen and I went up like a torch. My hair was now on fire, flames surrounded me and I started to scream both from pain and in fear. I remember my eldest daughter Catherine, then eight years old, running towards me and I remember my mother-in-law pushing her out of the way, fearful that she too would catch fire. Somehow I had the presence of mind to go back into the kitchen and grab a towel and my mother-in-law wrapped it tightly around me. Later she said that her most frightening moment was when she started to remove the towel only to see flames start up again.

The next few hours passed in a haze of agonised impressions. My husband drove me to hospital, smoke still rising from my hair. All I could do, half-fainting from pain, was to speak in tongues. In the emergency room the nurses covered my back and arm with sterile pads and poured water on my back for a couple of hours. Each time the cool water would bring a moment's relief but the heat radiating from the burn evaporated the water within seconds.

Finally a doctor injected me with morphine, bandaged me up and sent me home with a good supply of pain-killers. I was to return in three days later for them to assess how deeply the burns had gone.

The following morning a friend came round to visit me and brought me a word of encouragement from the Song of Solomon which said this: 'Your name is ointment poured forth.' (Song of Solomon 1:3 NKJV). She believed that as I spoke the name of Jesus over my burns that His name would act as a healing ointment. Amidst the trauma and shock of what had happened I received that word and, being a songwriter, I turned that promise into a song that I sang over and over again in faith. Today I have one tiny scar under my left arm that reminds me of the goodness of God and no other scarring at all from that incident. His name truly is ointment and that song was a song of power and deliverance for me.

'God is the chain breaker – as Paul and Silas sang praise, the chains that held them were broken and rendered powerless. That alone would be enough, but that is not where the story ends, the sung praise of Paul and Silas broke the chains and opened the prison doors of all prisoners within earshot of their singing. When we decide to open our mouths and put volume to the praise of our minds, we harness the chain breaking power of praise not only for our own lives, but for the lives of others.' **Ben Fielding**

A song of anguish

'Answer me when I call to you. O my righteous God.
Give me relief from my distress;
be merciful to me and hear my prayer.'
(PSALM 3:1 NIV)

Christians are not immune from suffering and loss. When we admit that fact in these songs we recognise that God is present in the dark times too and is listening to us. It is in these places of death that new life is given by God. There is great power in bringing our deepest pain, doubts and fears to God and refusing to pretend that everything is fine when it is not. There is great power in speaking to God rather than closing off from Him when times get tough. These are songs of faith because that sort of honesty and vulnerability implies a deep level of trust in God.

Jesus Himself, when He was dying on the cross, made the words of one of these songs of anguish His own when He cried out: 'My God, my God, why have you forsaken me?' (Matthew 27:46 quoting from Psalm 22:1 NIV) These may not be songs that we will sing in corporate worship but they are essential songs for our individual journeys of worship in the secret place.

'Those who sow in tears will reap with songs of joy

He who goes out weeping carrying seed to sow

Will return with songs of joy carrying sheaves with him." (Psalm 126:6,7 NIV)

A song of gratitude

'Thank you! Everything in me says "Thank you!'
Angels listen as I sing my thanks.
I kneel in worship facing your holy temple
And say it again: Thank you!'

Thank you for your love,
Thank you for your faithfulness;
Most holy is your name;
Most holy is your Word.
The moment I called out, you stepped in;
You made my life large with strength.'

(PSALM 138:1-3 THE MESSAGE)

————

These songs flow out of the songs of anguish. They celebrate the goodness of God in bringing the songwriter through and are marked by a deep thankfulness. There is a wonderful example in Luke's gospel when Simeon, who has long watched his people and their suffering and waited for the Messiah to come, finally holds Jesus in his arms and thanks God in a song. (Luke 2:29-32).

These are the testimony songs that we can write and that remind us of God's goodness to us. It's not just about being thankful for the dramatic interventions of God either. I had a friend who could take half an hour in prayer simply thanking God for the way the leaves moved in the wind; the warmth of the sun on her face; the comfort of the chair she sat on; the meals she was able to eat that day and so on. She taught me so much about gratitude for the daily blessing of God. There is great power in thankfulness because it deals with the sin of entitlement. Everything is grace.

————

A prophetic song

'The Lord says to my Lord:
"Sit at my right hand until I make your enemies
A footstool for your feet."
The Lord will extend your mighty scepter from Zion;
You will rule in the midst of your enemies.'

(PSALM 110:1,2 NIV)

————

This psalm of David's was later quoted by Jesus in reference to Himself (Mark 12:35-37)

Most of the prophetic books are written in poetic form even if they were not intended to be sung and David and others wrote songs that spoke prophetically both of things to come and that spoke into the life of their nation at the time. In the New Testament, Mary and Zechariah both sang prophetically of the implications of the birth of Jesus (Luke 1:46-55 and 68-79)

Graham Kendrick wrote an inspiring prophetic hymn a few years ago called 'O Lord the clouds are gathering' that looked at the state of the world and spoke of the ultimate triumph of the cross and the witness of the church. I believe that there is an important place for prophetic songs in our worship as long as they are submitted firstly to the authority of the Bible and secondly to the authority of the church leadership.

'I believe with all my heart, that when we bring these songs, they're not just random melodies, random lyrics, or random thoughts about a God who once was. I believe that the living God, Jesus, is breathing His life, is breathing what He's wanting to say, what He's wanting to do in this day and age, at this time in history, in this place, in and through His people. When we sing these songs, it's like the prophetic is cutting through the atmosphere. The prophetic cutting through culture, lighting the way, showing what God wants to do.[9]'

Joel Houston

9 Joel Houston – 'Broken Vessels Song Story' https://hillsong.com/collected/blog/2014/07/broken-vesselssong-story/#. WVSWSIiGOM8 14/7/2014 Used by permission

A song of remembrance

'How can we sing the songs of the Lord
While in a foreign land?
If I forget you, O Jerusalem,
May my right hand forget its skill.
May my tongue cling to the roof of my mouth
If I do not remember you,
If I do not consider Jerusalem my highest joy.'

(PSALM 137:4-6 NIV)

This is probably not a category that you would find in any book on biblical songs but I wanted to include it. The songs in it could come from any of the other categories but what they have in common is the powerful associations that they carry. The blend of words and music is very evocative and there will be songs in our life, either that we have written ourselves or that we listened to during a particular time in our life that will always have a special place in our heart. We must not elevate them to some unrealistic place and refuse to embrace new songs and nor can we insist that these songs should be significant to anyone else but I don't think that there is anything wrong in having certain songs that remind you of special times in your life when God ministered to you.

I think this is something of what the Israelites felt in Babylon when they were being taunted and asked to sing the song of Zion. The associations of these songs with their home made it too painful for them to sing them in exile (Psalm 137:1-4). However while I think that they were right not to sing their songs in response to taunts from their captors I believe that there is power in singing songs of home when we are away. As pilgrims in this world we know that our home is ultimately not here but in heaven and our songs of home can serve as reminders of where we truly belong (Hebrews 11:13-16).

One of my experiences came when I was in High School. I will never forget being asked on a few occasions to sing 'Silent Night' in German and totally unaccompanied, before the whole class. This was a highly embarrassing experience for a self conscious teenager and what made it worse was that my teacher would listen with tears rolling down her face. We did not know much about our teacher's life. To us she was just a middle aged woman with a quiet manner who loved 'Silent Night'.

What I learned later was that, as a child, she had been in a Nazi concentration camp and that one of her abiding memories was of the inmates singing 'Silent Night.' I don't know whether any of the rest of her family survived but I can only imagine the horrors she went through there. For her the associations of that song must have been both sweet and painful and, looking back, I am glad that I used to try to sing my best for her.

A song of trust

'I lift up my eyes to the hills
Where does my help come from?
My help comes from the Lord,
The Maker of heaven and earth.'

(PSALM 121:1,2 NIV)

The songs of trust that are found in the Psalms are the most loved psalms for Christians and have probably been set to music most often. We will look at them in more detail in the section on the Psalms. They can be powerful songs of faith in the face of difficulty.

One of the most memorable songs of trust I have heard was written by a songwriting student back in the 1990s. .Jenny came as a mature student who was already a highly qualified singing teacher and pianist and, when she graduated, she stayed on with us as a singing teacher. A couple of years later she was diagnosed with an aggressive cancer that ultimately invaded her whole body. As she fought for her life she began to record some of her songs, including one that she had just written although I did not get to hear it then. As the year went on she gradually began to lose the battle for her health and by the second half of the year she was in a hospice where I would visit her. She often mentioned this song that she had written earlier in the year and I kept meaning to listen to it. On one of the last times I saw her, the cancer had spread again and she accepted that it was time to let go. We talked again about this song and she said that it was still very much her song for this whole journey. She told me that although she had not received her physical healing she had received a miracle from God in that He had healed her heart and brought a new closeness with her family. She was dying in peace and in victory.

So finally I went and found the song and listened to it and we played it at her funeral. The recording only consisted of her voice and piano because she never got round to finishing her album but it was and is a powerful song. It is called 'In the whisper of a moment' and is a beautiful example of a song of trust. I want to finish this section by quoting a verse and chorus from it:

———

'You have delivered me from harm
Turned my storm into a calm
In the whisper of a moment
You filled my days with endless joy
Give me hope to love You more
In the whisper of a moment.
Chorus:
I cried mercy Lord and You were there
Mercy Lord You found me where
Your mercy Lord, Your mercy Lord heard my prayer'
(JENNY KEATING 'IN THE WHISPER OF A MOMENT' QUOTED BY PERMISSION OF THE AUTHOR)

———

'If ever there could have been a one way street it would be a song sung to God but He can't help Himself, He's always singing back.' **Benjamin Hastings‘**

A song of commitment

'Teach me your way, O Lord,
And I will walk in your truth;
Give me an undivided heart,
That I may fear your name.'

(PSALM 86:11 NIV)

Many of the songs in the Bible are songs of commitment to doing what is pleasing to God and living according to His commands. Often too they include recommitment after a failure to live up to God's standards (Psalm 51). These are challenging songs to sing and we do not sing them lightly but there is a place for them in worship as we seek to become more and more like the Jesus.

I have one final personal story to complete this survey of songs sung to God. A few years ago one of my students asked me to come to a worship service at his church because he was leading a segment of the night. I went, not really knowing what to expect since it was an Anglican church although one with a lively reputation. I can't remember how long we worshipped for but it was a couple of hours or more. Different bands and leaders headed up the various sections and the worship took different forms, some of which was quite formal but all of which was heartfelt. The congregation was seriously committed to worshipping and I soon forgot that I wasn't in my own church and became caught up in what was happening as we all delighted in God. As we neared the end of the night the atmosphere became more intimate and more charged.

What happened next I'd never experienced before or since. As we were singing, and I can't even remember what it was we were singing, I became aware of other voices that seemed to be emanating from the high ceiling of the building. I stopped singing and looked around but everyone was still lost in worship. I listened more closely and there were definitely other voices, the purest of sounds that were somehow above and separate and yet at the same time were blending with what was being sung below in the church. I'm not a person who has visions or dramatic spiritual experiences generally and I have no rational explanation for what I heard. But I felt convinced in my spirit that I was hearing angels singing. It was as if the angels could not resist joining in the worship of our amazing Saviour.   I spoke to a few people after the service and no one else had heard what I'd heard but I went home changed by it. I believe that I was given a tiny insight into what happens when we truly sing a song to God.

———

'The choir and trumpets made one voice of praise and thanks to GOD – orchestra and choir in perfect harmony singing and playing praise to GOD:
Yes! God is good!
His loyal love goes on forever!
Then a billowing cloud filled The Temple of God. The priests couldn't even carry out their duties because of the cloud – the glory of GOD! – that filled The Temple of God.'
(2 CHRONICLES 5:13,14 – THE MESSAGE)

———

SUMMARY

A song sung from our hearts to God is a song of faith. It is worship that is in spirit and in truth and it carries great power. Some of the categories that these songs loosely fall into include:

Songs of wonder
These songs lift us from our preoccupations to worship God simply because He is God.

Songs of victory
These songs can both celebrate past victories or build faith by celebrating a victory before we experience it.

Songs of anguish
These songs express a deep trust in God as we bring our times of darkness and despair to Him in all the rawness of the emotion that accompanies that.

Songs of gratitude
These songs thank God for every act of grace in our lives from the small to the great.

Prophetic songs
These songs, submitted as they are both to the Bible and to the discernment of leadership, speak prophetically to the church.

Songs of remembrance
These songs carry powerful associations and remind us both of God's goodness to us in the past and of the fact that we are on pilgrimage through this world.

Songs of trust

These songs face difficult times with a sense of great confidence in God.

Songs of commitment

These songs express both commitment and recommitment to doing what pleases God and to becoming more Christ like.

GETTING STARTED

On 'This I Believe (The Creed)'
(Matt Crocker, Ben Fielding)

'I remember sitting down with Matt Crocker and discussing the idea of writing a song around the Apostle's Creed. A brilliant academic and Anglican Church leader in our city (Dr. John Dickson) had written to us to request that our Hillsong writers make an attempt at doing so. Months later the first few lines of the chorus were written of what would become one of the most difficult songs I have ever worked on. I was passionate about staying true to the form and structure of the Apostle's Creed, though also to utilize a modern song structure that would hopefully carry these ancient unifying words into modern worship services. The song was an exercise in unity and collaboration and reminds me of the power of coming together in unity around what we believe to be most true, both believing in our hearts and confessing with

our mouth. What unites us is indeed greater than that which divides,
us, for we are united in the Name that is above all other names…
Jesus.'

Ben Fielding

'I'm always looking and listening for a subject that needs to be
expressed in song. I'm asking questions such as, "What does our
church need to be singing at the moment? Where is the gap in our
theology of worship at the moment?"… So, when it comes to facilitating
a corporate worship expression, one of the key things that inspire me
is that song that is just yearning to be sung; a need which beckons the
lead worshippers and songwriters to put these prayers, revelation and
petitions into song'

Darlene Zschech

'Our God is infinite, which means there is always something more to
discover and always a new song to be sung.'[10]

Ben Fielding

---

10 Ben Fielding – '3 questions a song writer should ask before writing another song' https://hillsong.com/contributor/ben-fielding/ 14/6/16 Used by permission

CHAPTER 3

QUALITIES OF
A GOD-CENTRED
SONGWRITER

After teaching song-writing for over a decade and working with numerous students over that period; writing my own songs and reading what other songwriters have to say about their craft I have come to some conclusions.

There are certain characteristics that writers of worship songs have in common with any other songwriter and I will be looking at many of those in this book. However I believe that the qualities described in this chapter are particularly relevant for the person who wants to write worship focussed songs.

These are qualities that can only come out of a life that is lived for and before God. They have little to do with knowledge and everything to do with relationship. Without them it is still possible to write songs for worship since the skills involved in song writing are not difficult to learn but the songs will lack that touch of authenticity. They will lack the breath of God that turns an ordinary song into an inspired one.

I am not claiming to have arrived at all of these qualities in my own life but I'm encouraged by what I heard a preacher say once. He said that we did not have to have arrived in order to be able to teach something, only to be on the journey. As one who has been on the journey for a while now I hope that these thoughts will help you on yours.

'A God centred song writer is also someone who brings their songs with open hands. In this I mean we don't cling to them too tightly. We work hard to make the song everything it can be but then bring it to the table and trust God with the outcome. This is often easier said than done.'
Hannah Hobbs

We recognise the source of our creativity

We have been made in the image of the Creator God and He is the source of our creativity (Genesis 1:26,27). What is more, we are told that, as Christians filled with the Holy Spirit, we have the mind of Christ   (1 Corinthians 2:10-16). This is a huge concept and I wonder if we have really grasped its implications. If we have the mind of Christ then we are able to access what God Himself is thinking by the power of the Holy Spirit.

It means that we should be able to think bigger thoughts than those who do not know Christ, however naturally gifted they may be, because we have the advantage of having the Creator of the world living inside us! It means that we should be innovators rather than copiers. It means that we should lead the way in creativity rather than running to catch up with what the world has to offer.

Paul said: 'Do not conform any longer to the pattern of this world, but be transformed by the renewing of your mind'. (Romans.12:2 NIV). One of the greatest musical minds of the past, Johann Sebastian Bach, was a committed Christian who dedicated every work he wrote to Jesus. He influenced and continues to influence composers around the world. He did not simply replicate what was already there but he carved out new ground.

We write out of relationship

We only have to look at the Psalms to see that every one of them is written out of relationship. Whether the psalmist is praising or lamenting, the foundation on which he addresses God at all is that he is in covenant relationship with Him.

David, perhaps the greatest songwriter of all, wrote this as an epitaph on his life: 'The oracle of David son of Jesse, the oracle of the man exalted by the Most High, the man anointed by the God of Jacob, Israel's singer of songs. The Spirit of the Lord spoke through me; his word was on my tongue' (2 Samuel 23:1-2 NIV)

For David it was all about his relationship with God. When he sinned it was God who he felt he had offended first and foremost (Psalm 51:4) even though his sin had hurt others. When he won battles he credited his victories to God (Psalm 18). Whether life was going well or times were tough the songs he wrote were all viewed through the prism of his relationship with God.

Our songs need to flow from that same awareness of relationship. In fact we are in a better position than David because the covenant we live under now is based not on the blood of animals but on the sacrifice of Jesus Christ. Jesus taught us that we can relate to God not just as Lord but also as Father and that, through the Holy Spirit, we can know an intimacy that is more precious and reliable than any human relationship. We can love and be loved by One who will never let us down; One who knows and understands us completely; One who accepts us unconditionally but Who is determined to see us become all we are intended to be.

Where do we find our worth and identity? John, Jesus' disciple, had a revelation about who he was that defined him for the rest of his life. In his gospel he describes himself on a number of occasions as 'the disciple that Jesus loved' (John 13:23; 19:26;20:2; 21:7,20) That phrase summed up his identity and worth.

We so often rely on labels. I could describe myself as a mother, wife, teacher, writer, pastor or friend but none of them mean anything compared with saying that I am one that Jesus loves. If I know that I am loved by the Creator and King of the universe then nothing can shake my sense of security and destiny. All other descriptions are temporary. I could stop being a pastor or teacher or I could lose my friends but Jesus has told me that He will never leave me (Matthew 28:20). That is a wonderfully secure place from which to live life, love others and write songs.

'You get closer to the Shepherd, you just obey the word.
You're not worshipping by singing a song, you're worshipping
by throwing your life on the altar…It all comes down to the
heart. Having an amazing song means nothing if your heart
is not lining up with God and seeking after God. At the end
of the day my name's not going to be remembered, God's is'
Marty Sampson

We place a high value on character

At the end of the Sermon on the Mount Jesus told a parable about two builders (Matthew 7:24-27). One built his house on rock and the other built his house on sand. When the storms arrived the house on the rock survived but the house on the sand was destroyed. Jesus' point was that when we listen to His words and put them into practice then we are building on a solid foundation.

Our talent will only take us so far. God is very gracious and will often bless songs written by people whose lives are not reflecting the behaviour, thinking and attitudes of a follower of Christ. However that cannot continue indefinitely. We may still be able to fake an experience of worship but it will lack both authenticity and anointing. We will be like the man who built his house on sand and ultimately what we have built will crumble because it has no foundation. We need character to undergird the gifts God has given us.

It is vital to maintain our integrity as people who live out what we write in our songs. Jesus was always very strong with the people He described as hypocrites which, in the Greek, means actors (Matthew 23:27,28). Our Christianity is not a game that we play in public while living however we choose in private.

Jesus, who was closer to His Father when on earth than anyone else has ever been, lived a life without sin. Nothing was allowed to get in the way of that intimacy and communication between the Father and the Son. I know that I will continually be in need of forgiving on my journey here on earth but my desire is to grow in character so that I will see God more and more clearly knowing that 'Blessed are the pure in heart, for they will see God.' (Matthew 5:8 NIV)

'I think a God centred song writer is honest, devoted, persistent and never proud. Or at least that's the goal.'
Benjamin Hastings

We write for the right reasons

People write worship songs for a variety of reasons and here are some of the bad ones:

Writing songs in order to make lots of money.

Writing songs in order to become famous.

Writing songs in order to show off our talent.

Writing songs in order to manipulate or to control.

Writing songs in order to push a particular doctrinal bias.

Below, in no particular order of importance, are some good reasons.

We write because we have something to say Jeremiah knew that feeling of having something that he desperately needed to communicate: 'Whenever I speak, I cry out, proclaiming violence and destruction, so the word of the Lord has brought me insult and reproach all day long. But if I say, "I will not mention him or speak any more in his name," his word is in my heart like a fire, a fire shut up in my bones. I am weary of holding it in; indeed, I cannot.' (Jeremiah 20:8,9 NIV) The sense of having a message burning with us is a compelling reason to write. There are times when I have experienced a continual restlessness until I have sat down and expressed what is on my heart.

'For me, writing songs feels like breathing. I feel compelled to write, and if I don't write for a few days then things just don't seem to be quite OK with the world, as if someone has turned down the oxygen in the air.' **Reuben Morgan**

We write to bring words of life Over the years songs have been a very important part of my journey. In times of darkness there have been songs that I have played over and over again, drinking in the truth and hope that they bring. I remember a time of depression after the birth of one of my children when my life line was a worship album that reminded me of what was true. I want to write songs that bring words of life to others.

Australian minister and songwriter Steve Everist put it like this: 'When the confusion of life and the weight of sorrow squeeze people into silence, it is the calling of the artist to bring to life those words which will free people. It is the calling of the artist to bring hearts frozen by the barriers of living into the warmth of God's presence. It is the calling of the artist to say what cannot be said, to dream what cannot be dreamt, and to believe when belief appears all but impossible. It is the calling of the artist to confront Church and people with God's heart.'[11] Steve Everist

We write to please God Ultimately we do not write for fame and fortune but to please and exalt God. If God has given us the ability to write songs then, when we write them, it pleases Him. There is a wonderful passage in the film 'Chariots of Fire' in which the sprinter Eric Liddell, a committed Christian who later became a missionary to China, told his sister why he kept running. His explanation was that God was the One who had made him fast and so when he ran he felt God's pleasure. It was not ultimately about winning Olympic medals but about doing what he was created to do. What have you been created to do? Are you doing it?

We write because we want to We need to avoid a utilitarian approach by which we always have to have a practical reason for writing. If we only ever write a song because there is a space on the new album to be filled or a service coming up that needs a song then, as valid as that might be, we have lost something important in our song writing.

Sometimes we should write simply because we are creative beings

---

11 Steve Everist (quoted from his notes with permission of the author)

and we want to create something even if nobody ever hears it. When we consider how much of creation is rarely, if ever, seen by any human eyes we get a sense of our Creator God who makes wonderful creatures simply for the delight of creating. If our song is only ever heard by our Creator then that is reason and audience enough.

We write to lead people into the presence of God Everything in a worship song must serve that end. The melody, rhythm and lyrics are not the message but merely contain it. Our goal is to help the congregation to express their hearts towards God and our words can either help or hinder that process. We need to understand and write for our congregation, nation and period of history. We have been put on this earth at exactly the right moment and we have a part to play.

'The journey homewards. Coming home. That's what it's all about. The journey to the coming of the kingdom. That's probably the chief difference between the Christian and the secular artist – the purpose of the work, be it story or music or painting, is to further the coming of the kingdom, to make us aware of our status as children of God, and to turn our feet toward home.' [12] (Madeleine L'Engle)

We desire to be excellent

Paul gives a great definition of excellence in his letter to the Philippians: 'Not that I have already obtained all this, or have already been made perfect, but I press on to take hold of that for which Christ Jesus took hold of me. Brothers, I do not consider myself yet to have taken hold of it. But one thing I do: Forgetting what is behind and straining toward what is ahead, I press on toward the goal to win the prize for which God has called me heavenward in Christ Jesus.' (Philippians 3:12-14 NIV) Excellence is not perfection or a competition with others but a journey to become better than I was before.

---

12 Madeleine L'Engle *Walking on Water* Waterbrook Press USA 1972 p.193,4

We refuse to settle for mediocrity It can be a temptation to settle for mediocrity and limit the potential of what we could write. Often we accept the first draft as unalterable with the excuse: 'God gave it to me'. God is blamed for some terrible writing! Part of the key to avoiding mediocrity is to learn how to accept and welcome constructive criticism.

There is a danger too that, because worship choruses have a short life we might not write them as carefully as we would something that is intended to last. However the church and, more importantly, God to Whom we sing these songs, deserves our best.

We are committed to developing our skills One important way in which we can develop excellence is to develop our musical and lyric writing skills. Work out what your weak areas are and seek to strengthen them. Do the same with the areas that you think are strong. There is always room for improvement.

'I write a lot of really average songs and I find that they're the killers because you can think that they're going to be OK. My view is that if it doesn't stir you then it's not going to be a great song. A bad song can be good in that it may have well-formed melody and everything in the song may seem right but if it doesn't speak then it is a bad song.' **Reuben Morgan**

We celebrate our uniqueness

It is important that we write out of who we are. We need to know ourselves. God has created each of us uniquely and it is this unique person that He has called to be a writer. As we write about what we know, that will have the ring of truth about it.

We write out of our revelation As worshippers we express most powerfully those things that we have a personal revelation about even if that revelation is still unfolding. For example, I may have a revelation of the cross but I can guarantee that in a few years that revelation will be far deeper simply because we never stop discovering the riches of God in our lives here on earth. But I don't have to wait a few years before I write my song. It is enough to be on the journey and to draw others into that journey.

We imitate Christ not other people Our goal should be to become more and more like Jesus, becoming conformed to His image (Romans 8:29) knowing that, by His Spirit, He lives in us (Colossians 1:27). Jesus demonstrated this principle of imitation perfectly. He did not spend His time trying to impress or convince. Instead, His words (John 8:28,29; 12:49) and deeds (John 5:19,20) were only ever what He heard His Father saying and doing.

We were not created to be poor copies of other people but to be imitators of Christ. Being like Jesus is never going to limit us because He is far deeper and far more creative than we could ever be. In becoming more like Jesus we become more completely the unique person and songwriter that God created us to be.

'I think we have always set out to write songs and create
a musical expression that is almost uncomfortable in its
uniqueness. Not for the sake of progression, or to keep pace
with whatever the trend-monitor says, but simply because I
feel like it's an essential aspect of what I believe worship is!
It's supposed to be costly, it should always cause us to step into
a place where our strength is made invisible in the complete
pervasiveness of His power in all that we do, and that involves
taking risks.[4]' **Joel Houston**

SUMMARY

As God-centred songwriters we:

Recognise the source of our creativity
We are made in God's image and have access to His creativity by the Holy Spirit.

Write out of relationship
This is where we find our identity and the intimacy that will colour our songs.

Place a high value on character
The gifts God has given us need to be matched with integrity.

Write for the right reasons
We do not write for selfish reasons but in order to say what is on our hearts; to bring life; to please God; and to lead people into worship.

Desire to be excellent
We refuse to accept mediocrity and are committed to developing our skills.

Celebrate our uniqueness
We write out of who we are and do not seek to imitate other people, only Christ.

EXERCISES

1. An inside look

Take an honest look at yourself in relation to the qualities described in this chapter. Consider these questions:

- How much do your rely on God for your creativity?
- How would you describe your relationship with God?
- In what ways does your character line up with your gift?
- What are your truest reasons for wanting to write?
- Do you sometimes accept 'near enough is good enough' when writing songs?
- How important is it to you to write authentically out of who you are?

2. A prayer

Write a prayer to God based on your answers to the questions above. Where do you think your strengths lie? In what areas do you need to grow or change?

CHAPTER 4

WRITING CONTEMPORARY WORDS AND MUSIC

'Why should the devil have all the good music?' sang Christian rock artist Larry Norman. He was echoing the sentiments of Martin Luther, William Booth and many others down the centuries who used the music of their time to set to the great truths of the church. Sometimes they would use contemporary idioms when composing their own music but often they would take existing popular songs and write new words to them, a practice that still continues. I have sung children's worship songs to the tune of 'Puff the Magic Dragon'; Pentecostal hymns to World War Two hits; classic hymns to English folk tunes and worship choruses to melodies lifted straight from the charts often with the barest of disguises.

Sometimes the marriage of words and music is confusing to say the least. My first experience of Christian words set to a popular melody was as a new Christian in 1973 at a Billy Graham crusade in London. I found myself singing the hymn 'There is a green hill far away' to the tune of 'House of the Rising Sun'!   It was bizarre to sing of the crucifixion of the Lord Jesus Christ to a melody that I associated with prostitution!

It does seem to make sense though that we should write our worship songs in a way that is relevant to those who are singing them now rather than trapping them in a musical time warp. However there are certain considerations to take into account.

'I believe music was created by God, for God; not just a particular style or genre…As humans, created in His image, we are allowed the privilege of participating in the sound, and I hold firmly to the opinion that ALL kinds of music, can and should be used for the glory of God!'
Joel Houston

THOUGHTS ON CONTEMPORARY STYLES

It is important to find our distinctive style and, for writers of contemporary worship, that is necessarily going to involve our becoming familiar with the music that is around us.

Music is morally neutral but context can be significant

The more we listen to music in a particular context the more it becomes associated with that context in our minds. We see so many examples of this when music is taken from its original context and used in advertising or as a film score or in propaganda of various forms. This can work both for and against us as worship songwriters. If a particular style of music is associated solely with a negative context we can, by setting it to Scripture, change the association and meaning that has been connected to that music. However that can take time and the risk is that we can confuse and alienate people during the process unless we are careful about how we do it. I remember, as a young Christian, coming across resistance to any sort of music with a rock beat because it was thought to be associated with demonic or sexually abandoned behaviour. It took a long time for rock music of any kind to lose that association so that it could be used freely in certain types of worship.

What we must remember is that music cannot direct our moral actions. We make a choice as to how we respond to music however much we are emotionally moved by it. A worship song may move us to tears but whether we act on those tears and truly worship is still a choice that we make. Ultimately it is what is in our hearts that matters rather than what comes from the outside (Mark 7:15)

Some musical styles date more quickly than others

The more specialised the musical style of the song, the more quickly it will date. This is not such a problem when writing worship choruses as they are only designed to have a short shelf life but it is more of a problem if you are writing a modern hymn or anthem that you hope will last longer. Notice how the hymns that are still sung, such as 'Amazing Grace,' have a classic simplicity about their melody and structure that have stood the test of time.

'I think that there are seasons and the styles of music and genres of music that you listen to change. You grow and change in life and that always reflects on what you read and what you listen to; what inspires you. So all of this will directly affect everything that comes out of you.' **Darlene Zschech**

Contemporary choruses still need to be both singable and playable

Not many of us are expert rappers for example and nor do we have the range of a Mariah Carey. We need to remember that we are writing for a congregation that is not made up of professional musicians and singers and so should adapt our material accordingly. The style you write in is also affected by the worship leader's voice and style of singing and wise songwriters remember that if they want their songs to be introduced at church.

We also need to be sure that contemporary styles are playable by the musicians on your team. The increase in popularity of electronic music means that certain genres require equipment or instruments that are not always readily available e.g. using tracks or building synth sounds.

The audience that you are writing for will affect your style

Different age groups tend to enjoy different types of music whether it is the Baby Boomer and rock or a teenager and EDM (electronic dance music). You may need to compromise on your natural style if you want to relate to your listener. Chris Falson, a successful writer of contemporary choruses, told one of my classes that, because he wrote for a church that liked a strong rock feel for its lively songs, he needed to respect that. He would have liked one of his songs to have a Latin feel but he chose instead to write it in a more rocky style in order to meet the needs of his audience. That is a true servant attitude. He was not concerned with showing how contemporary or sophisticated he could be but simply wanted to write songs that would be vehicles for worship for his church.

Successful contemporary choruses tend to avoid stylistic extremes

Successful contemporary choruses are actually usually a little behind the times musically. Our job as songwriters is to lead people into worship not into the latest musical style that has caught our fancy. There is more freedom if you are writing specifically for Youth groups since they will be more comfortable with the latest style but, if you are writing for the main adult congregation, you must be careful to educate gently rather than dragging them screaming and protesting into an unfamiliar and unsettling musical style. If you push them too far outside their comfort zone you will distract from worship rather than encourage it. After all it is difficult to worship if you are frantically trying to work out how to fit the words with the melody or how to syncopate your clapping without getting it wrong and making a fool of yourself. By all means stretch and educate a congregation but do it gradually and gently.

Experiment with contemporary hymns

A hymn is able to build on a theme through the verses which may then be summarised in the chorus and can serve to teach important truths which was particularly significant when a large proportion of the congregation could not read or have access to a Bible. However we could argue that it is still relevant today as many Christians tend to rely on the church service rather than reading the Bible for themselves. The music and the lyrics, while still being contemporary, will tend to have a more classic and timeless feel to them.

e.g. 'Man Of Sorrows' (Matt Crocker, Brooke Ligertwood). The image of the 'rugged cross' comes from an old hymn that has now been used in a contemporary way.

e.g. 'Cornerstone' (Jonas Myrin, Eric Liljero & Reuben Morgan, verses from 'The Solid Rock' by Edward Mote Traditional). The verses are not contemporary but the music and the chorus lyrics are.

e.g. 'No Other Name' (Jonas Myric, Joel Houston) Contemporary words and music

e.g. 'O Praise The Name' (Anástasis) (Marty Sampson, Benjamin Hastings, Dean Ussher) Contemporary words and music

On 'O Praise The Name' (Anástasis)
(MARTY SAMPSON, BENJAMIN HASTINGS, DEAN USSHER)

'…We began talking about the hymns and their timelessness, and how powerful many of those older songs are. 'How Great Thou Art', 'Amazing Grace' (among others) were mentioned and we set out to write something which would be written in the same genealogy as those inspirational songs.' **Marty Sampson**

Being contemporary applies to the words as well as the music

We will consider this in more detail later in the book but writing a song in a contemporary musical style using 16th century English really does not work. We can often be very particular about the particular musical style that we are using in our desire to relate to a contemporary culture and yet be very careless about our words. We are ready to admit that choruses written as recently as five or ten years ago have become dated musically but then we cling to the language of the King James Version. There is an inconsistency here that we need to address.

'Prosody requires that contemporary words coalesce with contemporary music. It is the responsibility of modern songwriters to continue to progress the sound of our song, tempered by a reverence for the ancient message for which we are entrusted. I personally would never chose to trade meaning for the sake of contemporaneity and I do not believe we need to.' **Ben Fielding**

Being contemporary does not mean plagiarising

Having said that the church in the past used the popular melodies of the day as the music for its songs we have to be aware of modern copyright laws, especially if we are planning to market our songs. If you take a Coldplay melody, set new words to it and record it you can expect big trouble! Even a memorable hook of a few bars is plagiarism if you have copied it exactly. Plagiarism may be the sincerest form of flattery but a professional songwriter will not see it like that if you pinch his music! Sometimes we can be tempted to be careless because we think that our song is only going to be sung in our church and no one will know that we have lifted someone else's melody. However be warned, songs have a way of getting around! And, quite apart from that, we are called to be people of integrity whether anyone is watching or not.

'Try to focus on where world music is not just church music…
You box yourself too much if all you do is listen to a few
bands…like a painter looking at only one landscape.'
Marty Sampson

Knowing a wide range of types of popular music can enrich your songwriting

The more widely you listen, the richer your music will become and the less likely you are to fall into the trap of plagiarising because you will not be reflecting one narrow style of music. I am a great fan of Sting's songs because he manages to draw from so many musical and lyrical influences and yet still sound unique.

Be careful though that you do not end up with something that is such a mix of styles and influences that it is unworkable. For example the long lyric lines of country music do not work with Latin rhythms. The key is to work out aspects of different styles will blend and create something fresh and new.

'Each song has a fingerprint. An identity. The greatest songs
are always set apart from other songs because they either
sound unlike any other song or they carry a message that is
being conveyed in a way that is completely fresh. The songs
with the most impacting fingerprint leave a print on everything
they touch.' **Matt Crocker**

Stay true to yourself

Don Francisco writes in a country idiom that is often despised by 'sophisticated' musicians and yet is greatly loved in many quarters. When he wrote an album of worship songs (High Praise 1988) he stayed true to his style and himself. I have no doubt that those songs were sung with great enthusiasm around the country where other types of music would have failed to connect with the congregation. His songs are no less contemporary simply because they happen to fall into a particular category and we have to beware the danger of trying to fit a certain mould when all we need to do is write the best songs we can in a way that will communicate with our 21st century church.

Although various elements may affect your style, the way to write the best songs is to write in a style that is comfortable for you and that you like even if it doesn't seem to be the most commercially viable style at the time. Sincerity counts for far more.

'I think honest writing never goes out of fashion. The opposite of cool is the person trying to be cool but it's funny how cool tends to catch up with the person who's just being themselves.'
Benjamin Hastings

SUMMARY

It makes sense to write songs that are relevant to the people who are singing them but there are things that we need to bear in mind about writing in contemporary styles:

Music is morally neutral but context can be significant.
Associations can mean that some music will be harder to use in worship.

Some musical styles date more quickly than others.
This is especially true of specialised sub categories of style.

Contemporary choruses still need to be both singable and playable.
Do not assume that your congregation or worship leaders are professional singers.

The audience we write for affects our style.
We should be writing songs that our congregation will relate to and enjoy singing.

Successful contemporary choruses tend to avoid stylistic extremes.
Stylistic extremes can be counterproductive when it comes to worship.

Experiment with contemporary hymns
Find the balance of contemporary and classic.

Being contemporary applies to the words as well as the music.
Archaic language can sound mismatched with a contemporary style of music.

Being contemporary does not mean plagiarising
Do not 'borrow' music from the charts for your songs.

Knowing a wide range of types of popular music can enrich your songwriting.
Work from a wide musical palette.

Stay true to yourself.
Write in a musical style that you enjoy and are comfortable with.

On writing for a new generation

'I think one of the biggest challenges in writing songs for a new generation is writing something that captures a listener's attention and has memorable qualities that resonate long after the song has been sung.

In addition, what this new generation needs more of is truth and depth. I believe they need to hear the Bible in a way that they haven't before. As songwriters a constant challenge is the ability to create new imagery and new analogies for describing the greatness of our God. Staying relevant doesn't always mean turning to the colloquial norms of the time, but I do think it means staying in tune with the culture that we are writing for.

In saying this, I believe an honest song that comes from
a songwriter's heart can go beyond all the rules and stir
others to let their guards down. The world is filled with so
many shallow and meaningless songs so when a song that is
vulnerable is presented, nobody can argue with it.'
Aodhan King

EXERCISES

1. Listen to different recordings of the same song

Take a well known hymn or chorus and listen to as many different recordings of it as you can find. Christmas carols can often be a good place to start as they are continually being reworked for a contemporary audience. Analyse what it is that is making the style contemporary.

2. Listen to a contemporary songwriter who writes in a variety of styles

Try to work out what the musical influences are on the songs. Work out what makes the songs still distinctively those of the songwriter.

CHAPTER 5

PRIME THE PUMP OF CREATIVITY

My husband spent his childhood in a little village in England and it was only in the 1950s that water was piped to the houses. Before that the villagers were reliant on wells that were operated by pumps. The way this worked was as follows: a bucket of water was always kept by the well and, before any water could be pumped from the well, this bucket had to be emptied into it. I'm not sure of all the technicalities but apparently this created a vacuum so that when the pump handle was worked the water in the well could be accessed. If water was not poured in then no more water could be pumped out but if it was poured in then there was an endless supply of fresh, cold water from the well.

Jesus told us that if we want to keep our life we must first lose it; that if a seed is to produce fruit it must first be thrown into the ground and die; that you can only keep what you first give away. It is the same with creativity. In order to prime the pump of creativity you must first pour something in and, just as with a water pump, creativity will begin to flow.

The hardest part is starting! Every creative person knows that feeling of staring at a blank computer screen, or canvas or sheet of manuscript paper. You know that you have something that you want to express and yet you seem unable to begin. Even experienced songwriters can suffer from 'writer's block' at times when inspiration seems to desert them. It is at these times that priming the pump becomes essential.

So, what has to be poured into the pump so that your creativity can flow out? There are a number of things, some of which may seem irrelevant at this moment but all of which will contribute to your creativity. In this chapter we will look at some essential ingredients to pour into the pump of the creative process along with various practical suggestions that may help you get started.

'We write from who we are at heart. For me, my daily reading and devotional time with God is everything because it is where I draw from as a songwriter. It may sound cliché, but my time with God is well that I draw from when writing. So, I think some qualities of a God centred song writer include a love for His word and a love for being in His presence each day.'
Hannah Hobbs

LISTEN TO GOD

There was a period in my life when I doubted my ability to keep coming up with creative ideas. It was at a time when I was writing a new musical every year for the college students to perform and was desperately seeking inspiration. I remember praying one morning and clearly sensing God's whisper to my spirit. He told me not to worry about finding new ideas because He was the author of all the stories and themes in the world and would give me all I needed. I still had doubts about my ability to execute these ideas well but, from that point, I knew that I need never lack for creativity as long as I kept listening to Him. Your songs will be a combination of what God is saying to you combined with your life experiences. Look for inspiration in:

Worship

If we are going to write songs of worship it is important that we ourselves are worshippers. Often it is in times of individual or corporate worship that God speaks to us.

Prayer

We need to become sensitive to the voice of the Holy Spirit who leads us into all truth. We need to take time to listen as well as speak in our prayer times. Often we do not take the time to be still and silent in our busy, noisy world.

Sermons

Listen to the themes that are being covered; a phrase or an insight. Your pastor will be listening closely to the leading of the Holy Spirit and will have a sense of where the church is heading. I have seen this happen again and again at Hillsong church as our senior pastor, Brian Houston, preaches sermons on themes that are often already being turned into songs by our song writers. In that way both the messages that are being preached and the worship serve to reinforce one another and so have a greater impact on the church. In recent times our senior pastor has occasionally used some of the songs as a jumping off point for messages so it can work both ways if the songwriters are hearing from God.

'I believe that if you hear a teaching long enough, your life begins to embody that teaching… Our lives are shaped by the Bible-based teaching of the church. I write out of that place and whilst I've written a couple of songs based directly off a message, I would say that it's more my life that has been shaped under the teaching.' **Reuben Morgan**

Testimony

So many of my songs, most of which have never seen the light of day outside my times with God, have come out of what has been happening in my life.

Scripture

Re-express the great truths of the Bible in contemporary, lyric form. Our themes are found in the Bible which is full of songs. Spend time in the Psalms; the New Testament hymns (Philippians.2:6-11; Colossians 1:15-20); the songs in Revelation; Old Testament songs such as the song of Deborah; or the songs in Luke Chapters 1 and 2. These songs give great insights into the ways in which we can and should worship God. For example we see that there needs to be a balance between songs that are purely God-centred adoration and songs that are concerned with his impact on our lives. We see too that God is interested in every aspect of our lives. We see that pain as well as joy can be expressed.

Creation

We can use images from God's creation to colour our lyrics. Often walking by the ocean or looking up at the stars at night can inspire songs as we consider the magnitude of creation.

The modern world

Re-express Biblical images in 21st century terms. Look at the world around you and imagine Jesus telling his parables now.

The liturgy

Look for inspiration in those moments in the service that would be enhanced by music. For example we could write a song for a special offering or for communion.

e.g. 'Beneath The Waters (I Will Rise)' (Brooke Ligertwood, Scott Ligertwood) - baptism

e.g. 'This I Believe (The Creed)' (Matt Crocker, Ben Fielding) - The Apostles Creed

The church calendar

Christmas, Easter, special occasions such as Mothers Day, church anniversaries, special children's services can all be times when we can find inspiration for a song.

e.g. 'O Praise The Name (Anástasis)' (Marty Sampson, Benjamin Hastings, Dean Usher) - Easter

e.g. 'Grace To Grace' (Chris Davenport, Joel Houston) - Easter

Other songs

We have a great musical heritage, especially in the hymns that have stood the test of time. They can spark inspiration for new songs.

e.g. 'Broken Vessels (Amazing Grace)' (Joel Houston, Jonas Myrin) The first verse of 'Amazing Grace' is used in the pre chorus set to a new melody e.g. 'Christ Is Enough' (Reuben Morgan, Jonas Myrin) The bridge uses words from an old chorus 'I have decided to follow Jesus'

DEVELOP YOUR SONGWRITING SKILLS

When God told Moses to build the Tabernacle he equipped the builders with both spiritual gifts and practical skills. Both are necessary for us as songwriters too.

'Then Moses said to the Israelites, "See the Lord has chosen Bezalel son of Uri...and he has filled him with the Spirit of God, with wisdom, with understanding, with knowledge and with all kinds of skills...' (Exodus 35:30,31 NIV)

This was true also of the psalmists who were inspired by God and then added their skills to that inspiration.

'My heart is stirred by a noble theme as I recite my verses for the king; my tongue is the pen of a skillful writer.' (Psalm 45:1)

Learn to play an instrument

Imagine someone who aspires to be a successful tennis player but who does not know how to hold a tennis racket let alone play backhand or serve. If he then went on to say that these skills were not necessary and that he could play perfectly well without them you would probably be pretty unimpressed.

However if you cannot play an instrument you will find yourself equally handicapped when it comes to developing as a songwriter. Being able to play an instrument is a great aid to creativity and the more skilled you are the greater is your freedom to be creative. A guitarist who can only play three chords is obviously far more limited than one who is more skilled. Learning to sing will also help you as a songwriter because, as you sing your own songs, you become more aware of what is singable and what is not.

Become musically literate

Imagine our tennis player again. This time he is planning to play a tennis match but has no idea of the rules. He does not know what the net is for or why there are white lines painted on the court. He has no idea of the points system or even that he is meant to stand the opposite end of the court from his opponent! You would not hold out much hope for success for him.

Equally we would find it amazing if a novelist were unable to read or write. Why should it then be any less amazing that an aspiring songwriter should think he did not need to know the basics of musical theory? There are always the gifted exceptions who get by without theoretical knowledge but the fact is that trying to be a good songwriter without any musical knowledge is like trying to win Wimbledon when you have no idea of the rules of tennis.

Study every aspect of song writing

If we return to our poor tennis player one final time we find that he has now mastered backhand and he even knows the rules but he still has no idea how to serve. He may win a few points now and then but he still won't become a champion. And this is where our analogy breaks down because, although we need to pay attention to every aspect of song writing whether it be melody, harmony, arrangement or lyrics we may decide that we will work with our strengths and find a co-writer to complement those with his own. A bit like playing doubles perhaps! Whether we decide to go it alone or to write with someone who has complementary skills we must not neglect any element if we are to write good songs.

TAKE YOUR TIME

Time is at a premium in our fast paced world but there are no short cuts to a good song.

Allow enough time

Any sort of creativity takes time. Sometimes we can write a song quickly but generally it is going to take hours or days. I personally think that taking days is better because you can sleep on it and then come back to it with a fresh eye.

Use your time effectively

Work out when you work best creatively and set time aside then. I am a morning person and so whenever I need to think creatively, whether it is writing a song, writing this book or preparing a lecture, I plan to do that in the early morning. My son, who is a visual artist, is a night person and will often work into the early hours of the morning very constructively when all I want to do is sleep. You can save yourself hours of frustration by working out when you work best. There is nothing wrong with working on your song at other times but then you would be better to work on fine-tuning it or working out an arrangement for it rather than being in the initial stages of creation.

'I definitely need to set time aside to write. Sometimes I have a day, or days, or a week, or even a couple of weeks. Usually a week or a couple of weeks is better for me because I find that if I'm not getting very far then I can do something else that will help to prime me.' **Reuben Morgan**

COLLECT THE BASIC TOOLS

There are certain items that are indispensable for the serious songwriter.

Writing materials

Carry a notebook or your phone with you so that when you have an idea you can jot it down immediately. Keep it beside your bed because often great ideas can come as you are drifting off to sleep and you will never remember them in the morning. Admittedly sometimes what seems like a great idea in the middle of the night is not so great when you look at it in the cold light of day but it's still worth writing it down just in case.

If you read and write music then have plenty of manuscript paper, preferably with the staves widely spaced so that there is room for your lyrics underneath. Have good pencils and cross out rather than erasing or tearing up your work. Often you will end up going back to your first thoughts. This is why working directly onto a computer can be a disadvantage unless you save your earlier drafts. An amazing computer programme that can do everything is nice but optional. If you write a great song then someone will produce it beautifully for you.

'Getting started can often be the hardest part of the writing process. It is a discipline that needs to be developed. Not every idea comes 'ready made' but it could lead to something wonderful. A bad idea can lead to a good idea, so don't disregard the simple act of putting 'pen to paper' and seeing where it leads' **Hannah Hobbs**

Recording equipment

With advances in technology you can make reasonable recordings just using your phone.

Books

Invest in some books on music theory and the rudiments of music if you are not familiar with them. A Rhyming dictionary and a Thesaurus can help you with your lyric writing.

Musical instruments

Access to a guitar or keyboard is essential for playing harmonies as well as melody.

KEEP WRITING

Sometimes it can be so hard just to keep going but it is vital and here are a few tips.

Don't keep revising as you write

Write your song without trying to perfect every line and nuance. If new thoughts occur make a note but do not spend ages going over what you have already written otherwise you may end up wasting time revising something that, when the whole song is written, is no longer relevant or needs changing because the song has developed in a different direction. Aim to write the whole song with relatively little rewriting as a first draft. Then revise! I will say much more about that throughout the book.

Don't give up after one song

The best way to develop your creativity is to be creative. Most prolific songwriters write many more songs than they use. Work on a song and, if it is going nowhere, set it aside and start on another. Stephen Sondheim, creator of many successful musicals, says that the first five musicals he wrote were his apprenticeship. That is a lot of writing!

Writer's block

As I mentioned at the start, nearly everyone experiences a time when the ideas seem to have stopped flowing and this can be very frustrating as you spend hours getting nowhere. At those times the best thing often is to change activity. Go away and do something else or else work on a different section of the song. Even something as simple as going to make a cup of coffee can sometimes break the stalemate. Often writers work on several songs at the same time so that, if one song stalls, they can turn to a different one.

SUMMARY

It is possible to stimulate the flow of creativity in the following ways:

Listen to God.
God can speak to you in a wide variety of ways

Develop your song writing skills.
Your capacity to be creative will increase as you develop as a musician.

Take your time.
Good songs take time and it is important to use your time effectively.

Collect the basic tools.
These include an instrument, some way of recording your song and reference books.

Keep writing.

We learn to write by writing so do not give up if your first few songs are not very good.

EXERCISES

1. Experiment with right and left brain thinking

- *Use the creative right side.* Brainstorm on the right to find the big picture, the images etc. This is where we need to start. Choose a common word or concept as your starting place (e.g. trust) and write that in the middle of a blank sheet of paper. Allow word associations and ideas to flow without thinking about them. Think pictorially in images as well as words. Follow progressions of thought and associations in a direction as far as they will go and then return to your original word and start again. Don't cross anything out.

- *Use the logical left side.* The left side of the brain makes key decisions. Use the left side to clarify your thoughts and to put ideas into logical sequence. Start planning. Ask the tough questions of the song and make sure that you are communicating your message clearly. Think about Bible verses and passages that speak about your subject. Analyse your images.

2. Experiment on your instrument

- *Improvise and record your ideas.* Often a new chord sequence or a melodic or rhythmic riff can be the beginning of a song.

- *Sing through the psalms or in the Spirit* as you play your instrument and see what comes out.

- *Switch instruments* Often when you get stuck writing a song with one instrument it can help to switch to another. The difference in the way that you play it and voice harmonies can often spark fresh ideas.

3. Experiment with songs already written

- *Try rewriting a classic.* Write new lyrics to it keeping the melody and structure. Then write a new melody to your new words. The advantage of doing this is that you will be working with a well structured song and the structure will remain the same.

CHAPTER 6

FIND THE BALANCE IN THE CREATIVE PROCESS

Imagine a tightrope walker navigating a perilous walk between two buildings. There is no safety net and everything depends on his ability to keep his balance on the wire stretched between the two structures. If he walks with his arms folded across his body he will almost certainly lose his balance at some point and fall off. What he needs to do is stretch out his arms in order to maintain his balance. However, if he only stretches out his right arm he will overbalance towards the right and similarly if he only stretches out his left arm. Both arms need to be extended if he is to have a hope of keeping his balance and reaching the other side in safety.

But what does this image of a tightrope walker have to do with writing songs and why do we need to be concerned with balance? Some verses in Ecclesiastes illustrate an important principle that applies to more than just theology: 'Do not be over righteous, neither be over wise – why destroy yourself? Do not be over wicked, and do not be a fool – why die before your time? It is good to grasp the one and not let go of the other. The man who fears God will avoid all extremes.' (Ecclesiastes 7:16-18 – NIV) In the footnotes a variant reading on 'avoid all extremes' reads: 'the man who fears God will follow them both' when speaking about extremes. Here then is the principle:

Balance both avoids and follows all extremes.

Let's return briefly to our tightrope walker. His arms reach out to both extremes but he walks the middle path between them. To lean too far one way or the other would be fatal. In theological terms, a heresy tends to develop when too great an emphasis is placed on one truth at the expense of another or when there is an over-reaction to a truth that is too strongly expressed. For example, many of the early Christian heresies were related either to stressing Jesus' humanity at the expense of His divinity or vice versa. Balanced doctrine embraces both the completeness of Jesus' divinity and His humanity without letting go of either or balancing too far towards one or the other. I hope this is making sense because it is a helpful principle when we consider how we write songs.

Songwriters, Christians, people in general may loosely be divided into two camps in the areas I am going to consider and will tend to emphasise one preference at the expense of the other. However, by embracing both extremes, we will become balanced in our creativity and hopefully, avoid the trap of camping at one extreme or the other. Not all of these areas involve paradox, in the way that considering Jesus as completely human and yet completely divine does, but they all represent extremes of approach that need to be held in passionate tension.

'If there is one word I could use to describe effective song writing, it's BALANCE. Great melodies, but easy to sing. Interesting chord changes, but not too many in one song. Simple lyrics, but profound thoughts. Balance.'
Marty Sampson

Find the balance between the Word and the Spirit

Without the Spirit we may write songs that are biblically sound but that are not speaking into the church's current situation. Without the Bible we may sense what God wants to say but, in our human fallibility, express it in terms that are not biblically accurate.

Some of us will naturally find our songs coming out of times of prayer or worship and need then to turn to the Bible. Others will find songs coming from sermons or their private study and then need to bring those ideas before God in prayer for confirmation.

The Balance. We are called to be people of both the Word and the Spirit. As Christians we want to be inspired and that means asking the Holy Spirit to speak to us and spending time waiting on Him for the message. Then we need to reach out to the Bible that acts as a check on the message. Everything must be measured by the yardstick of biblical truth.

Find the balance between the mind and the emotions

Writers who focus solely on the mind know exactly what they want to say and how to say it. But a powerful message that carries no feeling with it can lack any real connection with those that hear it. Unless we write from our own heart emotions we will not communicate and connect successfully in our songs.

Writers who rely on their emotions write songs that have strong emotional impact and are very real in terms of personal honesty. But emotion on its own without some lyric substance to it can be simply emotionalism that has no lasting effect on people. We must have some lyric substance to our songs.

The Balance. We have God-given emotions but we also have a God-given ability to think and reason and need to learn to write out of both. The best songs are the ones that stir both our hearts and minds. Emotion needs to be linked to content.

> *'Both intellect and heart are important, they must work together. The best songs get this balance right. They are carefully crafted and have a depth that has been tastefully woven into the 'feel' or emotionality of the music.'*
> **Ben Fielding**

Find the balance between objectivity and subjectivity

Objective writers can write beautifully constructed songs but they can become too focused on technique and structure. They have a clear plan for what they want to say and where they want to go but it lacks the spark of personal experience. They need to tap into the subjective experience that gives the passion and authenticity to the song.

Subjective writers draw on their experience but their lack of objectivity means that they fail to distance themselves from their song and the song can be too personal to relate to or be sung by a wide range of people. Their weakness also comes from the fact that they have an urge to write but with no sense of direction. If there is no direction or structure all the writer's energy is used up trying to work out what he is doing.

The Balance. The balanced writer has a plan and strategy but is prepared to adapt and make changes if that proves necessary. Nothing is set in concrete but there is a sense of direction as well as an idea and desire to write. We believe as Christians that there is a pattern in life. We believe that life is not simply chaos and coincidences even though we cannot always see the pattern behind what is happening to us. Our job as songwriters is to find the pattern in the experiences. That means that we embrace the subjective experiences that come our way and then move to the objective expression of them.

'The balance between our personal experiences and the truth that is the word of God is what brings others hope and reminds us of God's faithfulness in our lives.' **Aodhan King**

Find the balance between the words and the music

This is not the age old question of what comes first in writing a song: the words or the music? This is about finding balance so that both words and music serve to convey the message of the song. At the extremes the musician will tend to find his melody and even have it mentally arranged for a band before really knowing what he wants to say while the lyricist agonizes over every syllable but pays little attention to finding memorable music to carry his words. You may well know your strengths and weaknesses in this area already but, if you do not, they will soon become clear as you start to write. A blessed few are equally gifted in and passionate about both areas but most of us have to work harder at one than the other.

The Balance. Understand that a worship song is more than a poem set to music and it is more than a catchy melody with some vaguely Christian words set to it. Grasp both extremes. Care deeply about the music that you put to your words if you primarily a lyricist. Think deeply about the words that you are putting into the mouths of your congregation if you are primarily a musician.

So to reiterate the principle: **Balance both avoids and follows all extremes.** If we have truly understood this principle of balance we will avoid stressing one extreme at the expense of the other and, at the same time, will embrace the extremes of Word and Spirit, mind and emotions. Our creativity is expressed through both our minds and emotions. It finds its source both in the Word and through the Holy Spirit. Like the tightrope walker we hope to negotiate our path safely to the other side but it is a learning curve and it is hard sometimes to step outside ourselves to see whether we are leaning too far one way or the other. That is why we need to depend on the whisper of the One Who stands outside time and human limitations and Who can guide us safely through.

'The only doctrine that I have in music and in music making is that it basically comes out of the nature of paradox: that you have to have the extremes; that you have to find a way to put the extremes together; not necessarily by diminishing the extremity of each one, but to form the art of transition....You have to keep the extremes but find the link, always find the link, so that there is an organic whole.' Daniel Barenboim[13]

---

13 Daniel Barenboim and Edward W.Said, *Parallels and Paradoxes* UK 2002 p.68

SUMMARY

Principle: Balance both avoids and follows all extremes.

Find the balance between the Word and the Spirit.
Seek the inspiration of the Holy Spirit and test it by the yardstick of Scripture.

Find the balance between the mind and the emotions.
A strong emotional impact in our songs needs to be linked to solid content.

Find the balance between objectivity and subjectivity.
Draw from experience and then find the structure within which to express it.

Find the balance between the words and the music.
The words and music should work together to convey the message.

Aodhan King on writing 'Sinking Deep'

'The song started with the melody, which came together over the course of half an hour (this is definitely not always the case ha!) This part of the process is always an enjoyable one for me as I feel like the melody helps to set the scene and bring the emotional tone of the song.

When recording melodies (before lyrics) I like to sing words and phrases that naturally come out…After listening back to the voice memo I remember listening to the bridge and the first line that I sang was 'your love so deep is washing over me'…

The funny thing about this was that earlier that week I had been reading Ephesians 3:18…So it only felt right that I would base the song around the idea of being established and rooted in the deep love of God. From this point the lyric process seemed to be so much easier as the theme gave me so much room to move, but also a place to come back to.

The overarching tone of the melody was quite reflective and devotional so staying honest to those sensibilities was definitely important when writing the lyrics. One thing that really helped me was covering an A4 piece of paper in words that I liked and that I felt best represented the emotion I wanted to convey…

The process of this song taught me so much about being sensitive to the natural emotion of a melody, as well as the need for honesty and vulnerability in our lyrics. Without these things the songs are more difficult to write, but also may miss the message that you are trying to convey.' **Aodhan King**

EXERCISES

1. Listen to songs

Listen to a number of worship songs. Try to work out whether they lean more to one or other side in the four areas we have discussed.

2. Examine your own strengths and weaknesses

Think about each of the points in this chapter. What do you consider to be your bias in each case? What do you need to do to find the balance?

FINDING THE WORDS

On 'What a Beautiful Name'
(Ben Fielding & Brooke Ligertwood)

'The starting point for this song was the first chorus melody and lyric.
Quickly after sitting with Brooke, we had mapped out the structure of
this song, not limiting the song to just the beauty or wonder in Jesus'
Name but culminating in the great power that is in that Name. Brooke
and I laboured over the lyric, going back and forth over months,
through Bible verse after Bible verse, trying to poetically bring what
we were reading to life with new words. Though most of the song was
finished within a couple of days, my favourite lyrics came months later
when we had nearly given up. It is a lesson for me in the richness of
collaboration and the fruit of persistence, perseverance and rewriting
until every line of the song moves you as a writer.'

Ben Fielding

'Most of the song ['What a Beautiful Name']…was penned in a glorified cubicle in the suburbs of Sydney over a few days in December 2015. From there we spent months crafting the lyrics to riff on our core scriptures – Hebrews 1:1-4 and Colossians 1:15-20, 26,27 – yet be simple enough to make sense on a first reading.'

Brooke Ligertwood

'I like to start with a thought or a title ideally, even if it's just a couple of lines of lyrics that I really love. That helps me to frame everything else around that one main idea.'

Benjamin Hastings

'I love lyrics. I love their ability to give voice to the rich emotions of life that many millions cannot find ways to say what is in them to say. But this has always been the role of the artist, whether in song or script, colour or design. We need to dig deep to communicate what would be said by many if they possibly could.'

Darlene Zschech

CHAPTER 7

TELL THE TRUTH

'...truth has stumbled in the streets...'

(ISAIAH 59:14C NIV)

In our postmodern, relativist, individualistic world the words of Isaiah seem especially relevant. So often we hear statements such as: 'My truth is my truth and your truth is your truth' or 'we will get along just fine unless you try to insist on your version of truth'. In the name of tolerance, absolute truths are seen as the domain of the fanatic whether religious, political or otherwise. In fact, a claim to believe in absolute truths seems to be the one thing that our tolerant society cannot tolerate. Truth seems to have lost its footing, especially in our Western streets, and many would see that as a good thing.

But for those of us who follow the Lord Jesus Christ this attitude towards truth can never be our stance whatever the views around us may be. Jesus Christ described Himself as the Way, the Truth and the Life (John 14:6) and, if we are committed to Him we need to have a commitment to truth. Jesus not only is Truth but He told us that truth will set us free (John 1:14; 8:32) and that the Holy Spirit will lead us into truth (John 16:13). We must live as truth tellers (Ephesians 4:15) if we are to be like our God (Isaiah 45:19).

However as songwriters, sometimes out of enthusiasm, ignorance or even simply for the sake of the rhythmic feel or rhyme, we can end up blurring the truth in our songs. There is an incredible responsibility that goes with writing songs that may be sung in our own church and even around the world. Those who sing our songs may not have the experience to discern truth from error in our lyrics. If we value truth we will take great care to proclaim it especially as words and music together are so powerful. Martin Luther put it like this: 'Nothing could be more closely connected with the Word of God than music.[14]' (Martin Luther)

As I mentioned earlier, Robert and I have the task of checking the theology and clarity of all the songs that come out of Hillsong church and especially those that end up on our albums. This is huge responsibility and one that we do not take lightly. It is very rewarding to be a small part of the creative process of a song and very humbling at the same time as our songwriters, some with global reputations, submit their songs for review. That is not to say that we do not have some robust discussions on certain lyrics at times but it comes out of a deep mutual respect both for one another and for truth. Have we made mistakes over the years? We're only human and I'm sure we've missed lines that needed to be changed and been pedantic about changes that may not have been strictly necessary. However, I believe that, overall, the process has been hugely valuable.

---

14 Richard Viladesau *Theology and the Arts* Paulist Press USA 2000 p.25

'While most of us would feel a strong compulsion for veracity and accuracy in our lyrics, truth and accuracy can be elusive, lost not by intention but by lack of clarity. I have benefitted greatly from a robust lyrical proofing process, where my lyrics are tested by people I greatly respect, who objectively read only the words I have written, without any thematic preamble or musical recordings. It would be rare that we as songwriters will have the opportunity to preface our songs with a lengthy explanation of the background and meaning of the lyric we have written, so this process is vital. Our lyrics should speak for themselves.' **Ben Fielding**

TELL THE TRUTH DOCTRINALLY
(Hear what God is saying)

Because worship songs and hymns are so memorable it is especially important to make sure that our songs are theologically sound. Robert and I are sometimes called the 'lyric police' by our songwriters because we are so particular about this!

Our songs should be submitted to scrutiny

Jesus said only what the Father said and that is our challenge too. Everything we say must be submitted to the truth that is in the Bible. Once you have the core of the message then run it past other creative people to check its artistic impact but also run it past those with spiritual maturity and discernment.

Obviously there must be a balance here otherwise we can become paranoid that we are not stating the whole truth in every song. Songs are not meant to be theological lectures and are bound to stress one aspect of truth without necessarily balancing it but we need to make sure that what is being stressed is truth. For example I can write a song about the love of God without needing to speak about His justice and holiness as well. However what I say about God's love must be true.

An example of our process of scrutiny: 'Transfiguration (Brooke Ligertwood, Scott Ligertwood, Aodhan King, Taya Smith). One of the discussions that we had with the songwriters was over what it was that was revealed on the mountain of transfiguration and we agreed that it must be some aspect of Christ that was not already apparent to the disciples for them to react as they did to what they saw and heard. We looked at various options that the songwriters presented and considered 2 Peter 1:16-18 where Peter referred back to his experience of the transfiguration using words such as 'glory', 'prophecy' and 'majesty.' The final version the writers came up with in v.2 became 'Divinity confirmed in the transfigured word' and everyone was satisfied with that. Throughout this process, as has always been our experience, the writers were only concerned to write lyrics that reflected truth. Note: This has to be one of my favourite songs with its balance of retelling a significant moment in Jesus' life and then applying it so powerfully to our own lives as modern day disciples who are also on a journey.

On Transfiguration – Brooke Ligertwood, Scott Ligertwood, Aodhan King, Taya Smith

'This song is from Matthew 17:1-8. This is what we wanted to explore in this song – to take a narrative piece of scripture *and draw out the application and invitation within it. It was certainly a challenge to do – to take a story that is so specific and somehow make it a corporate worship song, but we thrived on the challenge and didn't try and rush it. It ended up taking three years to complete, working on it every now and then individually and then together in various configurations. Interestingly enough the four of us never sat in the same room when writing it!'* **Brooke Ligertwood**

Our songs should reflect the breadth of doctrinal truth

Although we cannot and should not try to put all of our doctrine into one song we do need to reflect the breadth of what we believe as a church over a period of time. This includes the nature and character of God, salvation, the incarnation, the life of Jesus and the message of the kingdom; the cross, the resurrection, Pentecost, the church and beyond including social responsibility and evangelism.

For example, some songwriters tend to focus exclusively on one aspect of salvation such as the cross and never write about the resurrection but we need to write about both. Reuben Morgan has written beautiful songs about the cross including 'At the Cross' and 'Calvary' but, he has also written powerfully about the resurrection as the authors of In their book 'The Cross is not enough' observed.

'Ross once spoke at a conference about the resurrection, in which five songs were chosen to match the conference's theme, all composed by Reuben Morgan of Hillsong. Among his best known compositions are "For All You've Done," "Mighty to Save," and "What the Lord Has Done in Me." In the latter song Jesus's resurrection is triumphantly confessed: "My redeemer lives...my Lord has conquered the grave." Perhaps one reason for Hillsong's

success is that the resurrection is celebrated in uplifting songs.'
[15](Ross Clifford & Philip Johnson)

Our songs need to tell the truth about God

When we talk about idolatry it is not just the danger of worshipping an object as if it were God but also of worshipping in ways that reflect an incorrect view of God. We need to make sure that we are worshipping the true God. The apostle John was concerned about false teachers who had a false view of Jesus that put them in danger of idolatry (1 John 5:20, 21). Their idol was not made of wood or stone but was a Jesus who they did not believe had come in the flesh and died a genuine human death (1 John 4:1-3). Of course, there is always the danger of worshipping worship itself which is also idolatry!

As songwriters we need to be clear in our portrayal of God so that we do not create a distorted picture. This can be hard for us as artists since there is something about the artist that does not want everything to be cut and dried in the way that a teacher does. We will talk about that poetic side later in the book but for now I want to stress the importance of loving truth as well as beauty.

e.g. On occasion Brian Houston, the senior pastor at Hillsong church has reminded the songwriters not to ask God to do what He has already done. The temptation as songwriters can often be to do this. We ask God to be with us or to send His Spirit when He has already done so. This sort of input is what we need to welcome from those in spiritual leadership over us.

---

15 Ross Clifford & Philip Johnson *The Cross is not enough* USA Baker Books 2012 p.98

TELL THE TRUTH EXPERIENTIALLY
(Understand your congregation)

Our songs will inevitably come out of our personal journey of faith but, if we are writing for a congregation, we need to be aware of where they might be in their faith as well.

We should tell the truth so that others can sing it too

Do not ask the congregation to lie! Be careful of making extravagant claims to love and discipleship that most people are not living. Sometimes when we write songs out of a time of great intimacy with God we can make statements that most of the congregation would find difficult to sing truthfully. A song that says something like: 'Whatever happens I will never walk away from You' would be very hard to sing with confidence. I hope that there would be no circumstance in my life that would cause me to walk away from God, even momentarily, but I cannot be absolutely sure of that. But if I sang 'Whatever happens You will never leave me' I would feel on much more secure ground both personally and doctrinally.

'As humans we find something strangely self-indulgent about pain but I think as writers, especially for the Church, it's our responsibility to elevate eyes above the small truths of their current situation and on to the BIG TRUTHS of the Word of God.' **Benjamin Hastings**

We should be careful about the promises we ask others to make

I don't want to make promises in songs that I might not be able to keep. The Bible warns us about making rash vows (Ecclesiastes 5:2-6). I want to be a person of my word so that if I say I will do something then I will do it. This is a principle that Robert and I as parents have always tried to follow with our children and it is a principle that I want to follow with God. Therefore statements such as 'I'll sell all my possessions and give them to the poor' may be true for you as a songwriter but it is a risky thing to ask your congregation to sing! Maybe this seems a bit picky but truth is important at every level and our words are very powerful.

What does this mean for us as songwriters? It means that we should think carefully about the words we put into our congregation's mouths. Obviously we don't want to be so careful that we end up saying nothing or only saying what the least committed person there would be able to say. Singing a lyric that says 'I'm prepared to worship you on Sundays but for the rest of the week I'll do what I want' is not really inspiring even if it may be true for a minority of the congregation. I am also aware that there will be people in church who have not yet made a commitment to Christ and for whom any songs of relationship would be beyond their experience at this point.

What we are trying to do is to avoid making promises or claims that are too far beyond the majority of our congregation. This will allow them to worship freely without feeling anxious about what they are singing or getting into the habit of singing words that they know they do not really mean. Remember always that we can sing songs that are beyond our experience to some extent as long as we are on that journey.

'I want everything I write to be based in Scripture, even if it is a prayer. I want to make sure that every line has biblical substance and integrity. That doesn't mean it has to be word for word Scripture but the tenor of my thought has to line up with the tenor of the word of God.' **Joel Houston**

TELL THE TRUTH EXEGETICALLY
(Set Scripture correctly)

'Do your best to present yourself to God as one approved; a workman who does not need to be ashamed and who correctly handles the word of truth.' (2 Timothy 2:15 NIV)

Setting verses from the Bible can be a powerful way of learning truth since we remember what we sing. We need to make sure that we have really understood the meaning of what we are setting. Here are some guidelines.

Choose your version of the Bible carefully

Every version of the Bible is a translation and there is no particular sanctity about any of them although you need to recognise the difference between translations and paraphrases. Choose the version that suits your song best which, if you are writing contemporary worship, probably means not using older translations with words such as 'thus saith'.

If you alter anything make sure that the meaning stays the same

It is all right to change word order, omit words, add words, repeat words or substitute different words as long as the meaning stays the same. In fact you will often need to change things as most of the Bible was not written to be sung and will not work well as a song without some adjustment.

However if you are not careful with your alterations you can end up saying something different from what was originally there and that can get you into serious trouble. A song that we used to sing had the line 'The first of all creation'. This had obviously been abbreviated from Colossians 1:15 'the firstborn over all creation' probably for the sake of the line length and number of syllables. However the change meant that it now implied that Jesus was a created being rather than the everlasting God who rules over creation.

Do not set verses out of context

Always check the context of any verses you set to make sure that by using the verses in isolation their meaning has not been changed. Years ago we used to sing a song based on Joel 2:9 and 15 which spoke of an army rushing on the city and blowing a trumpet in Zion. We would sing with great enthusiasm of the great army of God that carried out his word as if it were an army of deliverance for us. In fact, when I looked at the context I discovered that the army was God's army of destruction and judgment on sinful Israel and that the call was to repentance rather than rejoicing! Once I realized that I began to examine the context of the scriptures I sang more carefully.

Do not make a passage mean what it has never meant

Check your understanding of the verses you want to set with someone whose theology you trust. This is especially true of Old Testament passages. If there has been no New Testament reinterpretation of what a passage meant to its first readers then we must not change its meaning.

You might protest at this point that you are a songwriter not a Bible scholar but that is what commentaries are there for. Even something like a Study Bible can often prevent you from misunderstanding a passage and then using it incorrectly in a song. Remember that heresy is simply an aspect of truth that has been bent or distorted.

Here are some of the questions you need to be asking:

- What was the historical setting and who was the original audience?
- Who is this passage addressed to? This will affect the audience that you write for.
- Is it meant to be taken literally or is it using an image?
- What are the themes that it is addressing? You may want to look at other verses that develop the same theme for other parts of your song.
- Is the passage prophetic? Am I stretching the prophetic meaning in my song?
- In what way does it speak of Jesus? Always look for the redemptive, Christ message in what you read. It may point towards our sinful condition or it may point specifically to Christ but you need to find it for your song.

A great example of a combination of both theology and worship that has stood the test of time is the carol: 'Hark the Herald angels sing'. Here is the second verse:

———

'Christ by highest heaven adored, Christ the everlasting Lord;
Late in time behold him come, Offspring of a Virgin's womb,
Veiled in flesh the Godhead see, Hail, the Incarnate Deity,
Pleased as man with man to dwell, Jesus our Emmanuel!
Hark the herald angels sing, Glory to the newborn King.'

(WORDS BY CHARLES WESLEY,
MUSIC BY FELIX MENDELSSOHN – PUBLIC DOMAIN)

———

In this verse we have so many great truths of Christianity expressed. We sing of the deity of Christ; His historical appearance on earth; the miraculous virgin birth; the fact that He was completely God and completely man here on earth; and the encouragement that, if the angels worship and adore Him, then so should we. And that is only one of the verses. No wonder we are encouraged to sing 'Glory to the newborn King' and that this carol never fails to move us when we actually think about what we are singing. I want to write lyrics that both tell the truth and resonate with our hearts.

'When I wrote the song, 'My Hope', it was just after the horror of September 11th became reality. I really felt strongly to write a song that would help the Church in restoring certain ways of thinking, based on the truth of the word, not on feelings or circumstances. When I went to introduce the song, Brian Houston mentioned to me that he was starting a series on restoring hope. I went, 'You've got to be joking!" I couldn't believe it. And so, hand in hand, the Word and the worship sent a very clear and strong message to the Church that weekend. The feedback was incredible as once again the Holy Spirit had his way…I was challenged however, as I asked God the next week 'How many times have I actually missed moments like these?' **Darlene Zschech**

SUMMARY

We need to have a commitment to truth

Tell the truth doctrinally.
Make sure that your songs are theologically sound.

Tell the truth experientially.
Be careful about the words you expect others to sing.

Tell the truth exegetically.
If you are setting Scripture make sure that you do not change its meaning or take it out of context.

On 'Mighty to Save' – Reuben Morgan, Ben Fielding

'The original lyric read 'Everyone needs compassion, need more than religion'. Reuben and I were very pleased with the appeal to the relational nature of God; that we are reconciled not to or by empty religion but by a compassionate Saviour. While this is indeed true, we conceded in the drafting process that our intended meaning wasn't immediately clear, after all Christianity is a religion.

I never could have imagined just how impactful this song would be for our church and beyond. It is a constant reminder of this mysterious aspect of songwriting: after all of the hard work is done, we have to let go and trust God to do whatever it is He wants to do with our songs. It is also a reminder to me to continue to seek the heart of God for what it is that He would have His church be singing right now.' **Ben Fielding**

EXERCISES

1. Setting a psalm

Set either Psalm 9:1,2 or Psalm 34:1-4 to music. Choose your translation and then follow the guidelines in this chapter. You will notice that, even though the psalms do not fit with modern regular poetic metre, they are not very difficult to set to music. This, of course, is because they were originally songs.

2. Setting a piece of prose

Set either Romans 8:28 or John 3:16 to music. This is a much more difficult task because here you are trying to turn a piece of prose into a song lyric. You may need to rework it more but again be very careful to stay true to the original meaning.

CHAPTER 8

THE BASICS OF LYRIC WRITING

I love words. In fact my whole family loves words. Time after time our meals have been interrupted by one or other of us rushing off to find a dictionary in order to clarify exactly what a particular word means when it has come up in conversation. One of my husband's goals is to coin a new word that makes it into the dictionary! Without words we would have no vocabulary for our dreams.

Words are so powerful. God spoke creation into existence with a word and His Son is described as the Word. Words are the way in which God has chosen to communicate with His people and words are the way in which we communicate with Him and with each other. Jesus taught us that our words are extremely important (Matthew 12:36,37) and must be chosen with care. So when it comes to expressing our faith through words and music we need to understand the importance of finding the right words.

Poetry has been described as the best words in the best order and I believe that this is true of good lyrics as well. I think that songs that seek to express worship to God deserve our best efforts. We search for the perfect words to express what we want to say and then try to put them together in such a way that they communicate powerfully and clearly. Maybe it is an ideal that we can never reach but it is worth aiming for. This chapter seeks to introduce some basic concepts about writing strong lyrics. I need to warn you that it is a long one!

'I always ask myself: What is the key message of this song? And then bring everything into alignment with that.16'
Ben Fielding

FIND YOUR MESSAGE

Finding your message is all about working out exactly what it is that is burning in your heart and then expressing it in such a way that it connects with others.

Reflect the universal

We all share certain universal experiences. The same stories and emotions repeat themselves endlessly in human experience. The same great themes of love, loss, sacrifice, hope, war and death move people everywhere. We need to connect with those universal experiences and emotions.

---

16 Ben Fielding 'Writing Songs for Church: Q & A with Reuben and Ben' https://hillsong.com/collected/blog/2016/08/writing-songs-for-church-qa-with-reuben-and-ben/#.WVSfu4iGOM8 4/8/16 Used by permission

For example if I wrote a song that specifically thanked God for keeping me safe in childbirth more than half the congregation would not only not be able to relate to it but would feel positively awkward singing the words! However if I took that experience of God's protection and drew more general points from it then it would have a universal appeal. We all want to feel that Someone is watching out for us.

John Newton's beautiful hymn 'Amazing Grace' came out of his experience of salvation. However he did not refer specifically to his time as a slave trader because that would not relate to the majority of people singing the song. Instead he drew on his experience of grace to write a song that is still relevant to us all.

e.g. 'Desert Song' – (Brooke Ligertwood) came out of a difficult season for both of them but Brooke especially for her friend Jill who had tragically just lost her first child and who sang the song on the album with Brooke. However the lyrics reflect the universal experience of seasons of life whether it be the desert, fire, battle or harvest and the appropriate response of praise. It was a costly song both to write and sing but ultimately it was a powerful song of trust that we can all sing whatever trial we may be going through.

On 'Anchor' Ben Fielding, Dean Ussher

'I wrote a song called 'Anchor' with my good friend and writer in our church Dean Ussher. As we began to write, the line 'this hope is an anchor for my soul (Hebrews 6) was one of the first ideas that seemed to settle.

I looked up to see that Dean was clearly affected by that scripture. Dean and his wife had tragically suffered a

*miscarriage only a few months before and this scripture had
become a great reassurance in the midst of their loss and pain.
We committed to craft the lyric around Hebrews 6.*

*This song is deeply personal and yet it carries a timeless
message.'* **Ben Fielding**

Express reality

Write from your own faith experience because it is hard to be
convincing about something you have not grasped yourself. You
could argue that, if you are setting a passage from the Bible, then
you do not need to have experienced it yourself to set it and there is
an element of truth in that. Truth is truth wherever you find it and
some writers write gospel songs without any personal experience to
back it up. However worship is different. The worship songs that
we find in the Bible come out of deep personal experience and that
should be the template for us.

Think about your tone

What is the message that you want to convey? Your song should
express a clear attitude or emotion. Do not be vague or confused.
How do you want the song to impact on those singing it? You need
to set this and then maintain it.

e.g. 'My Hope' (Darlene Zschech) was written after September
11th and the widespread insecurity and anxiety that affected so
many lives. The message of the song is that God is still God and so
we can put our hope in Him no matter what happens. The lyrics
reflect that consistent tone as they start with a declaration of who
God is and then encourage us as worshippers to rise up from the

uncertainty that surrounds us and put our hope in Him. It became a powerful statement for the church in an uncertain time. It sprang from the specific but articulated the universal emotion of hope.

'I wrote the song, 'What the Lord has done' for my brother. I had the choice to just go and write the song so that we could sing it only on the day of my brother's baptism…but I imagined the congregation singing it all the time while I was writing it. The thought of a congregation singing the song made me shape it in a way so that other people could sing it. It's just consciously involving other people all the time whilst still being personal. I can tell my story in a way that involves everyone else's story, or I can just tell it in a way that nobody will relate to.' **Reuben Morgan**

UNDERSTAND THAT A SONG LYRIC IS NOT A POEM

A poem is the completed product while a lyric is only part of a song. It should need music to complete it. If you say too much then nothing is left for the music to do. There are exceptions of course when poetry is set to music but still there needs to be room left for the music to contribute.

A song lyric needs to have an immediate emotional impact

Often a poem needs to be **seen** to be appreciated and understood. In fact if a poem is easy to understand on the first reading we tend to call it verse rather than poetry. However a lyric needs to have an immediate emotional impact, since it may only be heard once. This means that, even if some lines may need to be sung a few times for the depth of what is being said to sink in, the overall message need to be clear on the first hearing.

A song lyric should aim for economy

If your lyric is going to allow room for the music then don't take too long to say what you need to say. If one syllable will do then why use two? This takes time and planning and the patience to work and rework a lyric until it is saying exactly what you want it to say in as few words as possible.

Strong lyrics are generally built on short phrases rather than long rambling lines. Avoid using two words where one says it all e.g. very unique. Avoid words that do not add anything to your message e.g. almost, very, just, really. Always look for ways to tighten up your lyric in the interests of brevity and it will not only allow your music room but it will be more powerful in its impact

e.g. 'It used to be darkness/Without you/I lived my life in blindness/But now I'm found' - 'Sing (Your Love)' (Reuben Morgan) Reuben has left lots of space in his verse lyrics

e.g. 'There's no darkness in Your eyes/There's no question in Your mind/God almighty/God of mercy' – 'Let There Be Light' (Matthew Crocker, Joel Houston, Michael Guy Chislett, Brooke Ligertwood, Scott Ligertwood, , Jonas Myrin). The space left in these lyrics allows the congregation time to reflect on what is being sung.

'Great lyrics gives people the words they can't find for the feelings they can't express.' **Marty Sampson**

MAINTAIN A CLEAR FOCUS

A frequent problem that I used to encounter with my students was that they would come up with a great idea but then the lyrics would go all over the place. We would jump from topic to topic and image to image without a clear sense of what the major theme was or where the song was going. The problem was a lack of focus.

You should be able to summarise your song in a few words.

A good lyric should be able to be summarised in one short sentence. The title is a good key as to whether you know what the heart of your song is about. If you can identify the title of the song after the first hearing then you have probably worked out what your song is about. The title should sum up the overall concept and should not have too many words in it. If it has to compete with another equally strong phrase that says something different then that may reflect a lack of clarity in your focus. Here are some titles that sum up the message of the song well and all are found in the chorus. 'Hope', 'No Other Name', 'Cornerstone, 'Stronger'.

'Sometimes even beautiful and brilliant lyrics get lost in a song that has no clear thematic direction.' **Ben Fielding**

Ask questions of your lyrics

For instance make sure that your verses, if you have more than one, still relate to the chorus that will follow them or write new choruses. Do your lyrics make sense if you simply read them out without relying on the music to cover up any careless writing?

How does your song start? Beginnings are very important. Often we work on the chorus but can then be careless about the first few words. How you start sets the mood of the song. You could try a question, a request, a dramatic statement, an image, a situation etc. e.g. 'Who compares to you?' 'Magnificent' (Raymond Badham) This song starts with a question to hook us in.

e.g. 'Grace what have You done murdered for me on that cross?' -'Scandal Of Grace' (Matt Crocker, Joel Houston). This opening statement challenges our thinking with a question and then uses a very emotive word 'murdered' to highlight the unjust, judicial execution of Jesus.

e.g. 'Any crown I've ever worn I lay it down' 'You Are Worthy' (Darlene Zschech) Here is an intriguing statement.

e.g. 'Through waters uncharted my soul will embark' – 'Captain' (Benjamin Hastings, Seth Simmons) This draws us in with an image that continues throughout the song.

Does your song lyric make a journey? In worship you are not telling a story as such but you are on an emotional journey. You need to have a sense of development through the song and a sense of where you are going to end even though the song will be repeated when it is sung in a worship setting. This may be in terms of a tag that is repeated at the end or even new material that is only sung once. You may bring back a key word or phrase that you used at the start. Be careful not to start on such a dramatic high that you have nowhere to go. We will look at examples of song lyrics that go on an emotional journey when we consider song structure.

What is your perspective? Is your lyric coming from a 1st, 2nd or 3rd person perspective? Is it coming from a singular or plural perspective? Work out what you think would be best for a particular song.

First person (I or We) Writing in the first person makes the song speak for those who are singing it. This works very well for most worship songs.

e.g. 'With All I Am' (Reuben Morgan) and 'Captain' (Benjamin Hastings, Seth Simmons) are both 'I' songs

e.g. 'Emmanuel' (Raymond Badham) and 'Empires' (Joel Houston, Dylan Thomas, Chris Davenport, Ben Tennikoff) are both 'we' songs

Second person (You – singular or plural). Be careful when using this not to sound as if you are preaching at the other people in the congregation. Writing in the second person has pitfalls too if you do not establish who the 'you' is in the song and the connection between the singers and the 'you' (e.g. beloved to the lover). If the 'you' is Jesus then it is helpful to make sure that you mention His name at some point during the song so that it is abundantly clear even to visitors who the song is addressed to. Do not change the identity of who 'you' is during the song and especially not within a section or you will confuse everybody.

e.g. 'To You Alone' (Reuben Morgan) and 'Oceans' (Matt Crocker, Joel Houston, Salomon Ligthelm) are both 'you' songs

Third person. (he, she, it, they) This is the most objective viewpoint in that the singer stands outside the song as an observer recording events and emotions. It can work in more formal worship such as carols and hymns, especially those that tell a story.

e.g. 'While Shepherds Watched Their Flocks By Night' (Este's Psalmes) This tells the story from the point of view of the observer.

e.g. 'God So Loved' (Reuben Morgan) and 'No Other Name' (Jonas Myrin, Joel Houston) are both third person songs

Changing perspective. This can work if the change takes place at a significant place. That might be between the verse and chorus or in the final verse of a song that is a series of verses in order to make a point. It is also fraught with danger unless you are very clear about what you are doing.

e.g. 'The First Nowell' – switches from 3rd person to 1st person on the final verse when we are all encouraged to worship.

e.g. 'Let There Be Light' (Matthew Crocker, Joel Houston, Michael Guy ChislettBrooke Ligertwood, Scott Ligertwood, Jonas Myrin). The verses and chorus are 2nd person singular and addressed to God but the bridge moves to 1st person plural as the words become the words that we sing about ourselves.

e.g. 'Man Of Sorrows' (Matt Crocker, Brooke Ligertwood) The verses are 3rd person singular speaking of Jesus and the chorus is 1st person singular as the songwriter considers the effect on us of Jesus' sacrifice.

'Often the simplest songs represent the most amount of work. It can take a lot of work to make something feel simple and flow well.' **Reuben Morgan**[17]

KEEP IT SIMPLE

Some of the most powerful worship songs are very simple. It has been said that a sign of greatness is the ability to express complex concepts in simple language. The account of creation in Genesis is one such example. God inspired the writer to use language

---

17 Reuben Morgan – *'Writing songs for Church: Q & A with Reuben and Ben'* https://hillsong.com/collected/blog/2016/08/ writing-songs-for-church-qa-with-reuben-and-ben/#.WVShloiGOM8 4/8/16 Used by permission

that would portray the power and wonder of creation and yet that would use words that could be understood by every generation. He could have used modern scientific terms but they would have been unintelligible to every generation until our own and, to future generations, would seem hopelessly dated. Our challenge is to express our faith, which is both simple and incredibly complex, in an accessible way.

Aim for simplicity with depth

A song lyric generally has less than one hundred words and there may be even fewer words in a worship song so avoid falling into the trap of trying to say too much. Make sure that every word counts and contributes to the message of the song.

e.g. 'To You Alone' (Reuben Morgan). Reuben based his simple lyrics firmly in the Bible, married them to a beautifully constructed melody, and said some very profound things about the fact that one day every knee would bow to Jesus and every eye would see Him.

e.g. 'My sin was great Your love was greater' - 'What A Beautiful Name' (Ben Fielding & Brooke Ligertwood). That simple statement says it all.

Avoid religious jargon

Avoid obscure theological terms that will be meaningless to anyone but a scholar. Words such as 'propitiation', 'soteriological' and 'predestination', apart from being impossible to sing do not belong in a worship song. However there are always exceptions and Brooke Ligertwood proved that in 'Beneath The Waters (I Will Rise)' when she wrote 'Now here my absolution/Forgiveness for my sin'. 'Absolution' is probably not in the average Pentecostal congregation's vocabulary and yet she got away with it although she was teased a bit for it too!

Make sure also that your lyrics are accessible even to those who do not generally go to church. Try not to make them feel excluded or stupid because they do not understand what they are singing. Although some biblical concepts such as the blood of Christ may not be familiar to a visitor we will still sing about it because it is so important. It is our job then as a songwriter to make sure that the meaning is apparent within the song. If we sing about His blood for instance then include a reference to His death. The language of sacrifice is an alien concept in modern society and may need interpreting.

e.g. 'Man Of Sorrows (Matt Crocker, Brooke Ligertwood). The significance of the crucifixion is set out in the verses and chorus so that in the bridge the context of 'Now my debt is paid/It is paid in full/By the precious blood/That my Jesus spilled' is clear.

Use contemporary language

If your music is contemporary then your lyrics should be as well. Some songwriters fight to keep 'thee' and 'thou' because they think it is more respectful to God. But how would you would speak to the Queen or the President today? How do you speak to God when you pray? I doubt that any of you say 'Thou' because 'Thou' is no longer the polite form of 'you' and so you do not need to use it. If you do it immediately sets up a barrier between your song and the congregation who will not connect with your language.

At the same time, you need to avoid slang and colloquial expressions that may mean something to you and your immediate circle of friends or age group but could confuse or possibly even offend others in your congregation and may be completely meaningless outside your own culture.

e.g. One song written a number of years ago by members of our youth group talked about God's love being 'mad'. In the colloquial language of Australian teenagers at the time that translated as 'amazing'. However it did not mean that for many of our congregation, especially since we are such a multi-cultural church and the thought of how it could be translated when it went to other countries made it clear that we could not use the word. We had visions of Spanish-speaking countries singing of God's love that it was 'loco'!

e.g. 'Only Wanna Sing' (Aodhan King, Ben Tan, Michael Fatkin) This is a more successful use of colloquial language containing lyrics such as 'This is no performance/Lord I pray it's worship/Empty words I can't afford' and 'I can't imagine why I would do this all for hype' This is a song that is written for young people who are typically postmodern in their desire for authentic, honest, personal lyrics and, as such, it succeeds in communicating a heart for genuine worship.

'Sometimes there is a temptation to try and create lyrics that will impress or wow people but my encouragement is to write it how you would say it in everyday language. Of course there is always a need to dig for new ways to say things, so I do think there is a balance to be found in it all, but there is something powerful about writing lyrics in a similar way to how you would speak in a normal conversation or prayer with God. There is an authenticity to this approach which often makes a song easier for people to connect with.
Hannah Hobbs

Use appropriate language

In your desire to write contemporary, relevant and intimate language remember that you are singing to God. Language that speaks about Him as your 'mate' that you 'hang out with' is not appropriate language to use about the King of kings. Jesus calls us 'friend' but He is still our Lord. We call God, 'Abba', but He is still the Creator of the universe. There needs to be a certain formality about the language we use when we speak to God.

We also need to be careful about the language we use when expressing our love for God. I have had a few students over the years who have written songs that did not specifically name Jesus or God as the object of their love and who have used expressions that would have been more at home in a romantic love song. Now we can use the language of romantic love as long as we make it clear who we are singing to and as long as it does not become erotic. Remember that the Song of Solomon was written as a human love song and that, while we can draw from it parallels between the love of Christ the bridegroom for His bride, the Church, there are many sections that are quite unsuitable for putting into a worship song. Once again we need to listen to the Holy Spirit and our leadership to check whether we are crossing that line.

However sometimes a seemingly inappropriate word can be appropriate. It all depends on the context.

e.g. 'Even when the fight seems lost/I'll praise You/Even when it hurts like hell/I'll praise You.' -'Even When It Hurts' (Joel Houston). Using the word 'hell' in a worship song has provoked a lot of reaction around the world but, when Joel first submitted the lyric, we approved it immediately while commenting that he would get emails about it. The reason we approved it is that he was using the word appropriately within the context of suffering. Sometimes what we are going through can feel as if we are in hell.

'It's all about balance…surrounding more unoriginal lyrics with new ideas or articulation. You feel like saying 'glory to God'

but it's been said so many times and you think you're being unoriginal, and it's frustrating. But it doesn't matter how many times you hear it, it's still a powerful statement and it's what you want to say. So I've found that if you can surround an unoriginal lyric with a new idea or lyric it will shine new light on the old one and you find that all of a sudden, even though it's been sung so many times, it still seems fresh.' **Joel Houston**

Make sure that your words are worth repeating

Simplicity is different from triviality. Your song needs to be easily understood but not dull. A few, well-chosen words can have great power. Remember that your song will be repeated many times.

FIND FRESH WAYS TO EXPRESS THE MESSAGE

It is very easy simply to repeat what has already been written. But if you are going to sound distinctive then you need to see your faith through fresh eyes. Those fresh expressions will then stay in the mind and the heart.

Express old truths in new ways

Here are some examples of fresh language that attracts our attention while encapsulating great biblical truths.

e.g. 'There's no taking back the cross/No regret in what it cost' -'Let There Be Light' (Matt Crocker, Joel Houston, Michael Guy Chislett, Brooke Ligertwood, Scott Ligertwood, Jonas Myrin). Jesus willingly gave his life for us but it is expressed in a fresh way here.

e.g. 'I touch the sky when my knees hit the ground' -'Touch The Sky' (Joel Houston, Dylan Thomas, Michael Guy Chislett). The concept of laying our life down, 'Upward falling', as the song puts it, is beautifully illustrated in this line.

e.g. 'My wealth is in the cross/There's nothing more I want/than just to know His love/My heart is set on Christ/And I will count all else as loss/The greatest of my crowns/Mean nothing to me now/For I counted up the cost/And all my wealth is in the cross.' -'Crowns' (Michael Fatkin, Scott Groom & Benjamin Hastings)

'Jessie and I were in our first year of marriage....Our bills kept coming through and after a month of job searching and unsuccessful phone calls I was feeling disheartened and a little apprehensive about our depleting balance...It was during this time I went into the studio with a few close friends and out came the lyric 'My wealth is in the cross'....I've come to realise though that what God really gave me was a confession for all my seasons and I pray it's just as true now, on the far side of provision, as it was for me then. Should I have or have not, may my wealth be in the cross.'
Benjamin Hastings about 'Crowns'

Ban clichés

A cliché is a phrase that has been so overused that it no longer has any impact. This is true both for literal language and for images. I am not talking about biblical images or phrases, such as Lamb of God or King of kings, since they are truth rather than cliché however often we use them. What I am talking about is the way we can throw statements together without considering that they have been put together like that a hundred times before. If something flows really easily lyrically ask yourself whether it is because it has been written before.

e.g. 'Worthy Is The Lamb' (Darlene Zschech) Darlene wrote 'The darling of heaven crucified'. She had some criticism for calling Jesus 'darling' as an overly sentimental or romantic term to use for the Son of God. For me though when I first sang the song that phrase stopped me in my tracks. My initial reaction was probably similar to the critics but it only lasted a moment before the tears began to flow and I thought about how precious Jesus was to His Father and what it cost Him to send His Son to die for us. It was the unexpected word that forced me to think about what I was singing.

e.g. 'Everyone needs forgiveness/The kindness of a Saviour' - 'Mighty To Save' (Reuben Morgan, Ben Fielding). 'Kindness' is an unexpected word here that makes us think.

Use visual images

Try using specific images to bring colour to your lyrics rather than relying on theological terms. See your lyrics and make your listener see them too. Paint pictures with your words.

e.g. 'The Gift Of Love' (Amanda Fergusson) In a song I wrote about the cross I wanted to encapsulate the physical agony, the emotional pain of the crowd's betrayal of Jesus and the setting in a dusty, middle-eastern city. I wanted us to see Him as we sang so I wrote 'Loving face, marked with blood and tears and dust.'

e.g. 'Splinters And Stones' (Joel Houston, Michael Guy Chislett) The second verse conveys a powerful visual image as it references the account of the woman taken in adultery and relates it to our own lives.

'Grace/You saw the crushing weight my flesh deserved/You kneeled and wrote forgiveness in the dirt/And one by one my accusers walked away/With nothing left to throw they made a cross/And knowing only love could count the cost/You were there.'

'Verbs eat adjectives for breakfast, almost every time. Descriptive writing uses great verbs.' **Benjamin Hastings**

Use descriptive, active verbs

There are so many ways to say 'said' and each one paints a picture. For example, murmured, snapped, sighed, retorted, whispered, whined etc. There are so many words out there that can bring colour to your lyrics. Look for them. If you are struggling for inspiration try looking in a dictionary or Thesaurus.

e.g. 'And all humanity aches to find this beautiful love you give' -'Saviour' (Darlene Zschech) The use of the word 'aches' is so evocative.

e.g. 'You met me at the sinners' table/I found You waiting by the well/Unexpected/You are always there/Tracing all my steps' -'Shadow Step' (Joel Houston, Michael Guy Chislett). Instead of saying simply that we encounter God in unexpected moments a picture is painted that shows Jesus eating with tax collectors and sinners and encountering the Samaritan woman at the well. The use of the verbs 'met' and 'waiting' reveal Jesus' initiative in salvation.

e.g. 'And I will rise among the saints/My gaze transfixed on Jesus' face' -'O Praise The Name (Anástasis)' (Marty Sampson, Benjamin Hastings, Dean Usher). The use of active verbs 'rise', 'transfixed' evoke so powerfully the moment when we will finally see our Saviour.

e.g. 'Tearing through the night/Riding on the storm/Staring down the fight/My eyes found Yours/Shining like the sun/Striding through my fear/The Prince of Peace met me there/You heard my prayer.' - 'Prince Of Peace' (Joel Houston, Matt Crocker, Dylan Thomas). This chorus is simply alive with the energy of all the active verbs and beautifully conveys the activity of Jesus on our behalf.

SUMMARY

Words are important and worth taking time over.

Find your message.
Your message needs to be specific enough to be real and general enough to connect with others.

Understand that a song lyric is not a poem.
Lyrics are designed to be heard not read and so need to have an immediate emotional impact and to leave room for the music.

Maintain a clear focus.
Can you summarise your song in a short sentence? Does it make a journey?

Keep it simple.
Make sure that your language is appropriate and aim for simplicity with depth.

Find fresh ways to express the message.
Use words that paint pictures and bring new life to old truths.

EXERCISES

1. Turning the specific into the universal

- Write a couple of sentences that summarise a specific experience, either good or bad, in your life.
- Write another sentence that describes how God became a part of it. e.g. Did you have a miracle? Did you receive direction that helped you to make a decision? How did God comfort you in a difficult situation?
- Write one more sentence that puts your experience together with God's part in a way that anyone could connect to it. Remember that you are looking for the universal experience or emotion and that will involve losing some of the detail of your personal experience.

2. Maintaining a clear focus

- Look back at your sentence in the previous exercise that found the universal message in your experience. Now try to find a title for your song that could be the hook in your chorus.
- Write an opening line. Try writing a few different ones.
- Think about the emotional journey of the song. Plan in rough terms what you want to say in the verses and chorus if that is the structure you want to use.
- Decide on your perspective i.e. 1st, 2nd or 3rd person.

3. Expressing old truths in new ways

- Write your opening verse and focus on using visual images and fresh language. Be as outrageous as you want at this point. You can always tone it down.
- Now check that you have expressed truth. Check with the Bible.

CHAPTER 9

THE RHYTHM
OF WORDS

When we talk about rhythm we tend to think about musical rhythm and our minds go to drum beats and rhythm patterns but the fact is that rhythm is basically any sound that contains strong and weak beats in some sort of regular movement. Think about the world around you right now. A clock ticking has a rhythm as does your heart beat and, more importantly for this chapter, so does the spoken word.

As soon as you listen to a conversation you hear the natural rhythms of our speech in operation. On the printed page it may not be apparent but, even as you read this, you can

hear the strong and weak beats in your mind. If you read this sentence aloud you will automatically stress some syllables and not others.

In this chapter we will look at how to add interest to our songs with the rhythm in our lyrics and how to match that rhythm well to the music.

RECOGNISE THE RHYTHM IN WORDS

Try saying the following sentence with every syllable given equal emphasis.

'What a wonderful day for a party.'

If you managed to lose the natural accents you will have found that you sounded rather like a robot or a dalek if you are a Dr. Who fan! Now say it again as you would in normal conversation. Your strong accents will probably have fallen on the syllables that I have now shown in **bold** type with perhaps slight variations depending on where you wanted the emphasis to fall.

'**What** a **won**derful **day** for a **par**ty.'

If English is your first language you would not have had to think about where the strong accents should be. However when it comes to setting these same words to music we can often forget what comes naturally. So when thinking about lyric rhythm we need to:

Stay consistent from verse to verse in the number of accented syllables you use

This may seem obvious but it is something that often trips songwriters up. The key is to create a pattern of accented or strong syllables that will scan the same from verse to verse as the same melody will be sung to each verse.

For example let us imagine that we are writing some extra lyrics to the melody of 'Amazing Grace' since I assume that most of you reading will know that melody. On the first line of the first verse I have four accented syllables, again shown in **bold type.**

'A**ma**zing **grace** how **sweet** the **sound**.'

Therefore I now need to have four accented syllables on the first line of my new verse.

I could write:

This **grace** I've **found** so un**deserved**.

This fits well but what if I wrote:

This **grace** I've **found** is **all** I could **ever** have **hoped** for.

Theoretically I could fit the words into the melody but it would sound rushed and would involve losing the accent on one of the syllables that needs accenting. Or I could write:

This **grace** I've **found** is **good**.

Now I would have melody left over although this is better than not having enough.

Introduce variety in order to prevent the lyrics from becoming monotonous

Having understood that we need to keep the same number of accented syllables for each repetition of the music now we need to bring in some variety or our lyrics will become monotonous. We can do this in a number of ways.

Vary the pattern of unaccented syllables from line to line. As long as we keep the same number of accented syllables we can vary the number of unaccented ones.

e.g. 'One Way' (Jonathon Douglass and Joel Houston)

Verse 1 starts: I lay my **life** down /at your **feet** (3 unaccented syllables at the start)

Verse 2 starts: You are **always** /always **there** (2 unaccented syllables at the start)

It is only a tiny difference. One extra unaccented syllable at the start of verse 1 but it brings variety. The number of accented syllables remains the same.

Vary between starting on the accented or unaccented syllables This works well between verse and chorus or chorus and bridge.

e.g. 'Transfiguration' (Brooke Ligertwood, Scott Ligertwood, Aodhan King, Taya Smith)

Verse 1 starts: '**From** the cloud You **speak**' (Starts on an accented syllable)

Verse 2 starts: 'Divinity con**firmed**' (Starts on an unaccented syllable)

Verse 3 starts: '**Lead** my longing **heart**' (Starts again on an accented syllable)

The chorus starts with an accented syllable '**Holy** is the Lord' whereas the bridge starts with an unaccented syllable 'Now I **know**'

Vary the pace If you have a fast moving lyric in your verse you may want to consider allowing more room and fewer words in your chorus or bridge or vice versa.

e.g. 'No Other Name' (Jonas Myrin, Joel Houston). The verses move quite slowly with sustained notes on 'Name, fame, praise' for example in the first verse. Then the chorus moves more swiftly with many more lyrics fitted into the same number of bars and the bridge is even more insistent rhythmically with a greater number of accented syllables pushing the momentum of the song forward.

Bridge: 'The **earth** will **shake**/And **trem**ble be**fore Him**/**Chains** will **break**/As **heaven** and **earth sing**/**Hol**y is the Name/Holy is the **Name** of **Jes**us **Jes**us **Jes**us'

MATCH YOUR WORDS
WITH YOUR MUSIC

Some songs don't work because of a disconnection between the words and the music.

Match them emotionally

It is important that the emotion of the lyric fits with the emotion of the music. It is very hard to sing about the peace of God that passes all understanding to a heavy rock beat! Prosody is the appropriate matching of lyrics and music.

Match the accents

The accented beats in the music need to match with the accented syllables in the lyrics. For the sake of illustration we will call a weak, unaccented beat (da) and a strong, accented beat (**Dum**). If your music goes (da **Dum**) then your words need to do the same. Therefore 'to **you**' (da **Dum**) works but '**Je**sus' (**Dum** da) does not because the accented syllable comes first. If you set '**Je**sus' to a music that goes (da **Dum)** the congregation will end up singing '**Je**sus' with the accent on the wrong syllable. Not only does that sound unnatural but it will be very hard for someone listening to work out what is being sung. We have all been guilty of failing to match the accents at times but that does not make it desirable!

Remember that musical accents occur on the down beat, on heavily accented beats and on high notes and so take care to match your accented syllables with these. Remember too that verse to verse you need to match your accents.

e.g. Verse 1: 'I /**saved** my **love** for /**you**.' (The oblique lines represent bar lines so the next syllable will be stressed musically)

Verse 2: 'You /**came** to **my** res/**cue**' (Here, if the music is the same, the accent will now fall on the 'cue' of 'rescue' which would be wrong)

Make sure that you have enough music for your lyrics

Sometimes we can write lyric lines that have too many syllables to fit the music comfortably and the temptation can be to contract the lyric (e.g. 'twas). The effect of doing this is to rob your song of its contemporary feel by using archaic language.

Another solution is to leave out words altogether (e.g. instead of 'you broke my heart' you write 'broke my heart'.) This can work well and sound poetic if used carefully. Make sure that you do not leave out an important word though that will make nonsense of your lyrics. Perhaps the best solution of all is to put in the extra time to find lyrics that do fit well. The opposite situation, of having too much music for your lyrics, is not really a problem at all as songs benefit from having space in them. Occasionally you can put a word in your lyric sheet for clarity but you won't necessarily sing it.

e.g. 'We sing louder' in the bridge clarifies that we are the ones singing louder rather than telling God to but the 'we' tends to be understood rather than sung. ('Let There Be Light' –Matthew Crocker, Joel Houston, Michael Guy Chislett, Brooke Ligertwood, Scott Ligertwood, Jonas Myrin)

Try to keep to a natural word order

When you change your normal word order because it does not fit rhythmically with the music it tends to sound clumsy. 'You to my rescue came' may fit with the music but no one would say it in real life. We will talk later about poetic licence but for now make it your goal to keep your word order as close to normal speech as possible.

STRESS THE IMPORTANT WORDS

Put your important words where they will carry the most weight.

Use the ends of your lines wisely

The notes at the end of lines tend to be accented and held longer and so any word put there will naturally be stressed. Let that word then be one of the most significant words in the line rather than 'to' or 'of'. e.g. 'He took away my shame' is stronger than 'He took my shame away'.

Words sung on long, high notes will be stressed.

If you have written your lyrics first then you need to make sure that your melody emphasizes the important words. If you are writing words to a pre-existing melody be careful about the words that you write for the climax of the melody.

Not all syllables are equal

Some words take longer to say than others and so will slow down a line. E.g. 'God's love' (Dum Dum) takes longer than 'on a' (da da). This is partly to do with accented or unaccented syllables but it also relates to the complexity of lip and tongue movements that a syllable takes. Try saying 'love' and think about the number of movements that involves. Now say 'a' and you can see why one word takes longer to say than the other even though they are both one syllable words.

Therefore when you want emphasize a thought you could choose words that take longer to say. E.g. 'The words you spoke were releasing' or 'The words you spoke were a life line.' Even though 'releasing' has more syllables it takes less time than 'life line' which forces us to slow down. Obviously I am assuming here that you have not already written your music as that would also affect the words you use.

MAKE YOUR WORDS SING

This is very important if you want others to sing your songs. So many songs have failed because they were unsingable and often that is down to the words rather than the music.

Words with open vowel sounds and some consonants sing

Words with open vowels like 'life', 'way', 'see', 'high' or singing consonants that include l, m, n, ng are words that sing. Compare those with words like 'risk, dump, talk' that are very hard to hold a note on.

Make sure you have words that sing at the end of lines and on high notes

Singable lyrics are important at any time but most of all on the notes that really count. If you ask your congregation to hold a long, high note on 'sit' you will not be very popular.

e.g. 'Oceans' (Matt Crocker, Joel Houston, Salomon Ligthelm) 'Name', 'waves', 'rise', 'embrace', 'mine' end each line of the chorus and are easy words to sing.

Try to avoid putting consonants next to each other

This is especially true if you put words next to each other that end and begin with the same consonant. In one of my songs I wrote 'Doubt tormented.' This is very difficult to sing without turning it into 'Doutormented' which is what my poor singer did when I first presented him with these words. Try to avoid putting any consonants together as a general rule although that is not always possible. E.g. 'doubt persuaded' is still harder to sing than 'doubt invaded' where the consonant is followed by a vowel.

Remember that the message has priority

In your care not to make something difficult to sing make sure that you do not move away from what you really want to say. The three 'doubt' examples above were all versions of a lyric that finally ended up as 'Darkness fell, I saw the shadows closing in/And sudden doubt persuaded me that I was all alone/As truth was overthrown.'

The use of the word 'persuaded' was not the best one in terms of singability but it was the best for the message of a song that was about propaganda and manipulation.

e.g. 'Real Love'(Michael Fatkin, Hannah Hobbs, Alex Pappas) The title and hook 'Real Love' breaks the rules by having two words that end and start with the same consonant. That means that most people sing 'Realove' but somehow it works in an up tempo song and nobody seems to be confused by it. Maybe it is the exception that proves the rule!

SUMMARY

Words have a rhythm that needs to work with the music.

Recognise the rhythm in words.

Listen for the natural strong and weak accents in your lyrics and work with them.

Match your words with your music.

Make sure that your lyrics match the music in accent and emotion.

Stress the important words.

Important words will be stressed if they are put at the end of lines or on high notes.

Make your words sing.

Understand which words and sounds sing well but do not compromise the message.

EXERCISES

1. Working out weak and strong syllables

Underline the stressed syllables in the following lines from Psalm 96:1-3.

'Sing to the Lord a new song;
Sing to the Lord, all the earth.
Sing to the Lord, praise his name;
Proclaim his salvation day after day.
Declare his glory among the nations,
His marvellous deeds among all peoples.' (Psalm 96:1-3 NIV)

2. Adding variation

Write a second line to the one below that contains the same number of stressed syllables but which varies the number of unstressed syllables. The oblique lines show where the bar lines are.

Jesus /**you** are /**won**derful to /**me**

3. Work out the musical rhythm

Take the words in Exercise 1 and put note values under each syllable so that each line consists of 2 bars in quadruple time.

e.g.   **Sing** to the **Lord** a   / **new** **song**.
$1/4$ $1/8$ $1/8$ $1/4$ $1/4$ / $1/2$ $1/2$

4. Write your own lyrics

Using either your own or someone else's melody, write a simple lyric that applies the lessons learned in this chapter. Take special note of the marriage of words and music so that they flow well and the accents match.

CHAPTER 10

COMMUNICATING EFFECTIVELY WITH IMAGES

'Through waters uncharted my soul will embark
I'll follow Your voice straight into the dark
And if from the course You intend I depart
Speak to the sails of my wandering heart'
'Captain' (BENJAMIN HASTINGS, SETH SIMMONS)

We tend to use language in two ways: either literally or figuratively. When we speak literally there is no confusion about meaning as long as we understand the words being used. For example, if I were to say 'I'm feeling sad today' my meaning would be clear. My words can be understood at face value.

However as soon as I start to use images and more colourful expressions, which is what figurative language is, then the listener has to work a little harder to understand me. For instance, I could say 'I'm feeling rather blue today'. Most people would immediately recognise that I am talking about feeling sad but a child might well have a very different mental image and peer curiously at me to see if he could detect a bluish tinge! Even more confusingly I could use colloquial images such as 'I'm feeling as sick as a parrot' or literary images such as 'The black dog is on my back ' These take me even further from a literal understanding but still mean basically the same thing.

This, of course, is the great challenge of using images. The example that I started this chapter with uses the image of our lives as a ship and Jesus as our captain very effectively throughout the song but it cannot and should not be taken literally. In using images we assume that our listener shares a common understanding of the picture being painted but the more subtle or obscure the image is the more likely it is to be misunderstood.

Before we look at some keys to using figurative language effectively I need to stress that everyone is different. Not everyone sees life in terms of images and metaphors. You can be a good songwriter without using images all the time. It is simply another tool. You may look at clouds and write powerful lyrics that evoke their natural beauty or you may look at clouds and see castles and mountains and battle scenes. Both approaches are valid and neither one is better than the other. Accept who you are and remain fresh in the language you choose whether it is literal or figurative.

WHY USE IMAGES?

If images are open to misinterpretation why use them at all? What can images do that literal language does not?

Images provide us with a different way of describing God

There are two ways in which we can speak about God. One is to describe Him in strict theological terms. God, Who is beyond our understanding, is described as infinite, invisible, omnipresent, omnipotent, eternal or transcendent among other terms. The other way is to use analogy in which God is compared to something familiar in our everyday lives and this involves using imagery to help to paint a picture of an unseen God. By doing this there is a point of reference for us. We know what a father is while we have little idea of what it means to be transcendent. It is part of the graciousness of God that He wants us to be able to understand what He is like.

The biblical writers used images repeatedly in speaking about God. When Jesus spoke about God, He spoke, among other images, of a king, a father, a homeowner, a farmer. When He spoke about Himself He used images such as shepherd, vine, light, door or mother hen.

Images appeal to the emotions as well as the mind

Jesus could simply have told us that God cares about the lost and we would understand that with our minds. However it connects with our emotions when He tells stories about a shepherd leaving his flock to search for a lost lamb; a housewife turning the house upside down searching for a lost coin and a father watching for his wayward son and then running to greet him when he returns.

Images catch the attention and are memorable

Images, when used well, paint vivid and powerful pictures that stay in our mind and heart. When writing about the prophets Abraham Heschel said of the prophet's images that 'His images must not shine, they must burn.'[18] (Abraham Heschel)   Here are just a couple of burning images that Hosea uses to communicate his message.

'Ephraim is like a dove' (7:11) Hosea portrays Ephraim like a senseless bird fluttering for safety between Egypt and Assyria and straying from God; 'withered plant' (9:16) Ephraim is a blighted, withered plant that bears no good fruit.

---

18   Abraham Heschel, *The Prophets* Perennial Classics New York USA 2001 p.8

HELPFUL HINTS ON
USING IMAGES

Because imagery is both powerful but also open to misinterpretation there are a few points to keep in mind.

Understand that the image serves the message

Sometimes we can get carried away with an image and forget that it is only there to help to communicate the message of the song rather than being the whole point of the song. The image needs to add insight to the message rather than detract from it by being too showy or clever.

e.g. 'Broken Vessels (Amazing Grace)' (Joel Houston) The message of the song is that God has restored our broken lives. The image of the broken pieces now mended and now vessels to contain Christ is a simple one that flows through the song but is never over worked (2 Corinthians 4:7).

Recognise the difference between literal and figurative language

It is important to recognise whether the language being used is literal or figurative in order to interpret it effectively. Literal language is taken at face value. The start of Psalm 107 says: 'Give thanks to the Lord, for he is good; his love endures forever.' (Psalm 107:1 NIV) This is a literal statement and the meaning is clear.

Figurative language is not meant to be understood in its usual sense or reference. Hosea describes those under judgment in this way: 'Therefore they will be like the morning mist, like the early dew that disappears like chaff swirling from a threshing floor, like smoke escaping through a window.' (Hosea 13:3 NIV) Here we do not take this literally but we recognise the transient nature of those under judgment.

Make sure that your comparisons are realistic

Sometimes we can fail to consider whether our comparison is believable and will connect with others. For example, I could write: 'Jesus is my teddy bear' because I want to show that He is as comforting and close to me as my favourite stuffed toy but in fact the image trivialises and belittles who Jesus really is rather than being realistic.

e.g. 'Jesus Is My Superhero' (Beci Wakerley, David Wakerley). Jesus is compared to a superhero which works for children who love superheroes. The concept that is communicated is that Jesus is a force for good who can rescue them and defeat any foe.

Make sure that you are consistently literal or figurative in a phrase

There is a danger of moving from one to the other and writing something that either does not make sense or is comical as in 'I ride the bus safely to work with the Lion of the tribe of Judah'. You can move between literal and figurative in different sections of a song but need to make it clear what you are doing.

e.g. Worthy Is The Lamb (Darlene Zschech). In the verse the cross is described literally and then in the chorus we have the image of Jesus as the Lamb so there is no confusion.

e.g. 'Your Word' (Chris Davenport). The verses use literal language to describe creation and the power of God's word in our lives. Then the pre-chorus uses the images of the word as a lamp and a light (Psalm 119:105) and in the chorus compares it to a fire (Jeremiah 20:9).

Make sure that you keep your central image consistent

Let's go back to the lion image. If the Jesus is portrayed as the Lion of the tribe of Judah don't suddenly change the image to that of the Lamb of God. The two images communicate very different aspects of Jesus whereas in Psalm 23 when David changes his image of God from shepherd to host it is still that of one who protects and cares.

e.g. 'Empires' (Joel Houston, Dylan Thomas, Chris Davenport, Ben Tennikoff) This song has a number of images in it but there is a consistency in the picture of humanity. Words like 'silhouettes, reflections, shadows, portraits' all point to the final expression at the end of Verse 2 'Images of our Maker/Sinners called out as saints'. We are fallen image bearers who have been redeemed hence the language of 'empires of light and clay'.

Remember that imagery can be used to varying degrees in a song

You can use figurative language as the central device of a song, as in Psalm 23, or just in a line or two, as in Psalm 3 where God is described briefly as a shield but the rest of the psalm is fairly literal.

e.g. 'Captain' (Benjamin Hastings, Seth Simmons) In this song the imagery of our soul as a ship guided and steered by God is the central device and needs to be understood throughout.

Look for contemporary images that will re-express Biblical truth

I remember reading about the Wycliffe Bible translators who tried to express the image 'Lamb of God' to an Eskimo community that had never seen a lamb. Finally they settled for John the Baptist exclaiming, 'Behold the seal of God' and suddenly everyone understood the image as they thought of a spotless, innocent creature that so often ended up with its head crushed because of man's greed and sin.

In his book 'Bruchko' Bruce Olson illustrates beautifully this concept of using images that are relevant to the audience as he speaks of Jesus coming for the Motilone Indians to teach them to walk in God's trails and to tie their hammocks into Him. Images that mean nothing to us as Westerners but that brought salvation in the jungles of Colombia.

e.g. 'Aftermath' (Joel Houston) In the chorus of this song the lyrics speak of the crucifixion and what it means for us. 'In a moment of glorious surrender/You were broken for all the world to see/Lifted out of the ashes/I am found in the aftermath.' In our 21st century world the language of aftermath is powerful and poignant with its meaning of the period that immediately follows a usually ruinous event e.g. the aftermath of war or a terrorist attack. Joel turns it on its head so that the apparently ruinous, disastrous event of Jesus' crucifixion is now good news for us.

'A song is another medium of communication, so what good is it if no one can understand what it is you are trying to say through it. Especially when you are trying to write a song that will lead others into the presence of God.' **Matt Crocker**

DIFFERENT TYPES OF FIGURATIVE LANGUAGE

There are various ways of writing figuratively, not all of which are suited to choruses, and I have listed some of the more useful ones below along with their descriptions and a few specific examples.

Personification

In personification, inanimate objects or abstractions are given human qualities For example, Zechariah.11:2 speaks of trees wailing and Psalm 114:3,4 speaks of the sea fleeing and the mountains skipping like rams.

e.g. 'Mountains bow, nations tremble' - 'Let Creation Sing' (Reuben Morgan)

e.g. 'The oceans and skies lift up their voice' 'Let Us Adore' (Reuben Morgan)

Apostrophe

In apostrophe an absent, or dead person or thing is addressed as if alive and able to answer. It is important to be clear about whom you are addressing and to be consistent. Jesus did this when he addressed Jerusalem: 'O Jerusalem, Jerusalem, you who kill the prophets and stone those sent to you, how often I have longed to gather your children together, as a hen gathers her chicks under her wings, but you were not willing.' (Matthew 23:37 NIV)

e.g. 'Scandal Of Grace' (Matt Crocker, Joel Houston) v.2 starts 'Death where is your sting/Your power is as dead as my sin'. The song draws from Paul in 1 Corinthians 15:55 who in turn draws from Hosea 13:14 and all three use apostrophe.

Simile

A simile compares dissimilar things using 'like, as, than.' When analysing the effectiveness of a simile or a metaphor note both the differences and points of similarity. The dissimilarity catches our attention so that we look for the similarity. Jesus rarely spoke about the kingdom of God without resorting to some sort of analogy to try to help His disciples. For instance He compared the kingdom to a mustard seed (Matthew 13:31) to illustrate the contrast between the tiny beginning that the kingdom has in the person and ministry of Jesus and its final fulfillment at the end of the age just as a plant starts as a tiny seed and grows large.

e.g. 'You broke the night like the sun/And healed my heart/With your great love.' – 'Take All Of Me' (Marty Sampson) e.g. 'Your love O Lord/Is like the oceans/Deeper than endless seas' 'Highest' (Reuben Morgan)

e.g. 'Like the wind/You'll guide/Clear the skies before me/And I'll glide this open sea/Like the stars/Your Word/Will align my voyage' 'Captain' (Benjamin Hastings, Seth Simmons)

Metaphor

A metaphor equates dissimilar things without the softening effect of using 'like' or 'as'. This tends to create a more striking effect. Jesus used metaphor when he said: 'I am the true vine; and my Father is the gardener.' (John 15:1 NIV)

e.g. 'There's a light in the darkness that shines giving hope to all the world'; 'There's a door that's been opened to all into a new and living way'; 'There's a fire that burns in our hearts to see the lost return' from 'Jesus The Same' (Raymond Badham). All the metaphors that Raymond has used here have biblical origins.

e.g. 'Your Name my hope/Fortress in the raging storm'; 'The Stone the builders rejected/Laid to ransom a fractured bride'; 'My life is Yours a living stone' from 'Mountain' (Matt Crocker, Joel Houston) Again these metaphors are all biblical in origin.

Symbol

A symbol often involves the whole song. Often one symbol conveys a second, broader one. For example light symbolises revelation. (John 1:5-9; 8:12)

e.g. 'Let There Be Light' (Matthew Crocker, Joel Houston, Michael Guy Chislett, Brooke Ligertwood, Scott Ligertwood, Jonas Myrin). Light as a symbol of revelation and cleansing permeates this song.

e.g. 'Every burning star/A signal fire of grace' from 'So Will I (100 Billion Times)' (Joel Houston, Benjamin Hastings, Michael Fatkin) Here the stars symbolise the gracious act of God in creation.

Allegory

In allegory the apparent meaning of the characters or events is used to symbolise a deeper moral or spiritual meaning. As songwriters today we need to find contemporary

allegories. Who is today's leper or Samaritan? Probably allegory is more suited to a gospel song than a chorus but I have included it because it is commonly used in the Bible.

COMMON ERRORS IN USING IMAGES

You may now be planning to fill your songs with metaphors and symbols. However, before you do so, here are a few common errors to avoid.

Mixing metaphors

Take care not to switch from one image to another midstream. For example: 'You are my strong tower who leads me beside still waters.'

'Another tool for the Director's palette.' I heard this on a 'Making of…' programme!

Using too many metaphors at once

If you do you'll end up with what is known as 'purple prose'. This is writing that is overloaded with competing images. Ben Fielding kindly gave me permission to use an example of mixed metaphor that he wrote for songwriting classes!

Song for Robert

(MY HUSBAND BECAUSE HE HATES MIXED METAPHORS!)

Verse

I stand on the field of who you are
You are the air above
The air below me
And I am shipwrecked on the shores
Of who you are
You break the daylight and the dawn
Here within me

Verse

In the trial and the rain
You light a fire
Like the wind you will illuminate me now
All I am for all you are
You are the one that I am for
And I will hold you even if you let me go

Chorus

I will run
Coz I am dancing
And I will fall
As I dance again
In the storm

Verse

Never once have I strayed from you
Though I fall I'm holding on
And like a rock
I am cast upon you
And to the field once again I will return

Bridge

Nothing can extinguish this living water in my heart
Nothing can shatter the fragile state of all you are

(REPRODUCED WITH PERMISSION OF THE AUTHOR BEN FIELDING)

There is so much wrong with this song that I will not attempt to describe it but leave it to you to critique!

Overworking the image

Remember that an image makes the point but it is not the message. If you lose sight of the message because you are so enamoured of your image then you have lost focus.

Being too obscure

Unlike a poem that is read a song is heard and may only be heard once. It does not matter if the listener does not grasp everything in the first hearing but the central message must be clear. There is a fine balance between writing a banal and obvious song and writing something that is so obscure that you need notes to understand it!

Misunderstanding or misusing a biblical image

When using a biblical image remember that the images reflect the culture of the time and so we need to work out what it would have meant to the readers of the day. This is where commentaries and Bible dictionaries become very useful. Even a familiar biblical image such as shepherd meant something very different back in David's time.

Misunderstanding or misusing an illustration from nature

God speaks to us through creation but what He says still has to be translated into words if we want to internalise the lessons. We also need to check that the lesson we think we are learning from nature is actually biblical. Remember too that nature is fallen and its lessons are not uncorrupted revelation in the way that the Bible is. For example, we can learn from the ant in terms of industry but should we be learning from the praying mantis in terms of mating habits?

Using an irrelevant image

We need to think about our audience when using an image. Some images are unintelligible to an audience simply because they are totally outside their experience. For example, using an image based on Quantum physics in a children's song or using an image based on an aspect of Western society in a remote jungle village.

Using a confusing image

Occasionally we can write a line that nearly works but, when we analyse it is actually confusing.

e.g. In 'Not Today' (Joel Houston, Matt Crocker) the original lyric of the 2nd line of the 2nd verse was 'Tell me, did all hell freeze in panic as You rolled back that rock'. Our feedback was that the problem with referring to hell freezing is that it naturally links to the saying 'That will happen when hell freezes over.' The implication of the saying is that whatever is being spoken about will never happen because hell will never freeze. As a result the natural answer to the rhetorical question in the lyric line would be 'No, hell did not freeze in panic' which is not what the songwriters wanted to communicate. The revised lyric that they came back with to us was 'Tell me did the darkness cry mercy as you rolled back that rock' which communicated exactly what they wanted to say.

SUMMARY

Figurative language is powerful but can lead to misunderstanding if not used carefully.

Why use images?
Images appeal to the emotions and are memorable as well as giving us a way of speaking about God that connects with our everyday experience.

Helpful hints on using images.
Use realistic, consistent, contemporary images that will serve the message of the song.

Different types of figurative language.
Understand how to use personification, apostrophe, simile, metaphor, symbol and allegory effectively.

Common errors in using images.
Stay relevant, clear, simple, biblical, truthful and economical in your use of images.

EXERCISES

1. Metaphors and similes

Think about the following metaphors and similes.

'You're like the rain that falls/Fall on this heart and make me new.' 'Need You Here' (Reuben Morgan) Write down some ways in which Jesus is unlike rain and then think about the similarities. What makes the image work?

- 'Like the wind/You'll guide/Clear the skies before me/And I'll glide this open sea/Like the stars/Your Word/Will align my voyage/And remind me where I've been/And where I am going.' 'Captain' (Benjamin Hastings, Seth Simmons) Write down the points at which God is not like the wind and the Word is not like the stars and then think about the similarities.

2. Writing your own images

- Write a song lyric that uses at least one image.
- Try to use something that you have not seen used in a song before.
- Ask questions of your image. In what ways is it like the thing that you are comparing it to? In what ways is it different?

CHAPTER 11

EFFECTIVE USE
OF RHYME

M ost of us grew up singing nursery rhymes and playground chants. Without consciously trying to learn them we can probably still recite the words even if it has been years since we last sang them. I found that, as soon as I had children of my own, words such as 'Jack and Jill went up the hill to fetch a pail of water/Jack fell down and broke his crown and Jill came tumbling after' came flooding back into my head. Why is it that, when we so easily forget many other far more important facts, we remember these songs?

We could point to a number of factors such as the simple melodies or the fact that we relied much more on aural memory before we could read but one very important element is that most of these songs use rhyme and rhyme sticks in the mind.

'Rhyme can help make the metre skip quicker, or it can make the song feel cheesy. Too much rhyme is not a good thing but too little rhyme and it becomes art and not as easily singable. There has to be some 'predictability' about your lyrics. The rhyme is a tool for people to remember the song. And if they remember it, they will sing it and really 'get' the message easier.' **Tanya Riches**

QUESTIONS ABOUT RHYME

Before we look at how to use rhyme in our lyrics we need to answer a few questions.

What is rhyme?

Two or more words are said to rhyme when each contains the same final **accented** vowel and consonant, and a different consonant preceding that vowel.

e.g. slave/brave, cling/bring.

The rhythmic accents of the words must match.

e.g. 'tender' and 'refer' have the same final vowel and consonant but the accent in 'tender' comes on the first not the second syllable.

It is easy to pair words that look like rhymes on paper but do not sound like rhymes.

e.g. find/wind; through/tough, naked/baked.

Only sound is important in rhyme not spelling.

e.g. bronze/swans is a rhyme although it does not look like one.

Why use rhyme?

Rhyme makes a song easier to remember

Rhyme creates a sense of balance Rhyme is closely linked to lyric rhythm, especially at the end of lines as the repeated sound creates a sense of balance.

Rhyme reinforces lyrically the musical principle of repetition Music relies on repetition and contrast and rhyme does that for the lyrics.

Rhyme stresses the important words We remember the words that rhyme.

Rhyme makes it easier for the listener to work out what is being sung We tend to cut off our consonants and so rhyme can help us to work out what we are hearing. For example, if you hear 'I will si-' and not the end of the word it could be 'sit, sing, or sin'. But if the rhyming line ended with 'bring' then the word is likely to be 'sing'.

When should we use rhyme?

Rhyme should be kept to a minimum otherwise it can become silly or comic. This is especially true of 2 and 3 syllable rhymes that can end up trivializing a song. e.g. follow/hollow/wallow.

The shorter the lyric line, the more noticeable the rhyme is and the more danger we can be in of over rhyming. For example if I wrote:

———

In love you came
And took the blame
I'm not the same
'Cause you took my shame

———

Apart from the fact that I have just written some uninspired lyrics you can see how the short lines emphasise the over rhyming.

Which words should rhyme?

Because we remember the rhymed words make sure that they are significant ones. Hopefully we will already be placing our important words at the end of the lines where they carry more weight. Rhyming them adds even more weight to them as we see in the hymn 'When I survey'

———

*'When I survey the wondrous **cross***
*On which the prince of glory **died***
*My richest gain I count but **loss***
*And pour contempt on all my **pride**.'*[19]

(ISAAC WATTS)

———

What is an identity?

An identity or homonym is where the two words have the same preceding consonant. For example 'loud/allowed, give/forgive are both identities. There is nothing wrong with putting these words together but they cannot be said to rhyme since they sound exactly the same and the result is rather flat if you have been using rhyme up to that point.

What is a rhyme scheme?

A rhyme scheme is the pattern of rhymes in a section. If we look back at my woeful over- rhyming we will see an example of an AAAA rhyme scheme since every line ends with the same rhyme. 'Came/ blame/same/shame' are examples of an AAAA rhyme scheme.

There are a large variety of possible rhyme schemes and you do not necessarily have to use the same rhyme scheme for each section in a song. In fact it is a good idea *not* to use the same scheme

———

19 Isaac Watts *When I survey* Public Domain

between verse and chorus in order to introduce some variety. Popular rhyme schemes include: AAAA, AABB, ABCB, ABAA, ABAB, AAB, AAAB/CCCB, AABCCB. 'When I survey' has the pattern ABAB.

What is near rhyme?

Near rhyme is very common in contemporary music as a whole. We will look at it in more detail later as it is a very useful technique in worship songs where exact rhyme can quickly become tired because the songs are repeated so much. Examples of near rhyme include: died/life; come/run; fine/time; ask/hearts/past.

TECHNIQUES OF RHYME

There are a number of techniques that we can use in order to make rhyme more effective in our songs.

Exact rhyme

Rhyming on the strong accents

1 *rhyme* = the rhyme comes on the last syllable of the line. It doesn't matter how many unaccented syllables come before it. Love/dove, complete/defeat, misinform/thunderstorm are all 1 rhymes.

2 *rhyme* = the rhyme comes on the 2nd to last syllable. E.g. follow/hollow, action/faction

3 *rhyme* = the rhyme comes on an accented syllable followed by two unaccented ones. E.g. muttering/stuttering.

Rhyming on the weak accents

There are a number of very sophisticated techniques here that belong more in a book on writing for Music Theatre so I will only look at a couple that we might possibly want to use in our worship songs.

Internal rhyme This is a rhyme that occurs within a line rather than at the end and can be quite satisfying if it is not overdone.

e.g. 'Crowned in **glory** creation a**dores** You' 'I Adore' (Reuben Morgan)

Trailing rhyme. In this a one syllable word is paired with either the first syllable of a two syllable word or the first of two words to make a rhyme. E.g. give/living; took/look up

Near rhyme

Near rhyme is all about making sound links between words. These words do not rhyme exactly but they have sufficient similarities to connect them in our mind. This can be a very satisfying technique to use because it is more subtle than exact rhyme.

Assonance

uses echoed vowels that create a sound link without using rhyme.

e.g. 'form/scorn; grave/grace' 'Gift Of Love' (Amanda Fergusson)

e.g. 'need/breathe' 'More Than Life' (Reuben Morgan)

e.g. 'You remain the same' 'You Are Worthy' (Darlene Zschech) Here Darlene has used sound links within the line.

e.g. 'Heaven is open, death is broken' 'Yours Is The Kingdom' (Joel Houston)

e.g. 'Name/waves; rise/mine' in the chorus and 'borders/waters; wander/stronger' in the bridge 'Oceans' (Matt Crocker, Joel Houston, Salomon Ligthelm)

Unaccented rhyme

The final syllable of both words rhyme but they are unaccented. E.g. given/heaven

Consonance

This is also known as half rhyme. In consonance the final consonants are the same but the preceding vowel sound is different. Wilfred Owen, a poet from the 1st World War, used this device extensively in his poetry. E.g. word/Lord, escaped/scooped. Consonance is a useful as it gives many more sound links between words. For example 'love' has very few exact rhymes and not many of them are that helpful e.g. love/dove/glove/of/shove. However if you are using this technique then there are some very interesting pairings that you can make. E.g. love/prove/gave/give/grave/starve etc.

Para rhyme

In para rhyme the first and final consonants are the same but there is a different vowel in the middle. E.g. moan/mourn, stir/star.

Augmented rhyme

In augmented rhyme a consonant is added to the rhyming word. This can enrich the rhyme as the listener gets more than he was expecting.

e.g. 'soar/Lord' 'There Is Nothing Like' (Marty Sampson)

e.g. 'sin/sing' Verse 2 'Scandal Of Grace' (Matt Crocker, Joel Houston)

e.g. 'stars/hearts' Verse 1 'No Other Name' (Jonas Myrin, Joel Houston)

Its counterpart, diminished rhyme, does the opposite and can be risky as the listener may be confused by what he hears because he gets less than he expected. For example if the first word is 'around' and that is paired with 'down' the listener, who is expecting a 'd' sound at the end may mishear 'down' as 'downed' or even 'drowned'.

PROBLEM SOLVING WITH RHYME

We need to be aware of some of the problems that can arise with rhyming.

Some 'don'ts' in rhyming

Don't weaken the end of a line or verse for the sake of a rhyme If you can't find a good rhyme consider another word; a near rhyme or no rhyme. The message is more important than the rhyme.

Don't twist your word order so that it sounds unnatural for the sake of a rhyme

Don't mix old and new English words for the sake of a rhyme e.g. 'you' 'thee'

Don't use clichés Use fresh pairings of words. Rhyme is an asset when it intrigues us but is boring when it is predictable.

Don't settle for near enough is good enough if you are using exact rhyme If the rest of your song has rhymed exactly a near rhyme can sound careless.

Don't rely too heavily on rhyme. Rhyme does not translate into other languages and so, if your lyric interest is entirely in your rhyme, then you will lose all of it once it is translated. Use rhyme to add to your lyrics rather than as the major focus of them.

Some 'do's' in rhyming

Be aware of traps of slang and pronunciation. Some words may not actually rhyme in another setting. A well known example from 'Manhattan' by Rogers and Hart makes fun of this fact but also makes its point when 'spoil' is rhymed with 'girl' ('goil' in a strong New York accent!)

Be aware that some words do not have a rhyme Try to avoid words that have few rhymes at the end of your lines e.g. love. Some words have no rhymes in the English language. Try finding rhymes for 'orange, angel, refuge, softly'.

Make sure you rhyme accented syllables e.g. If you rhyme 'free' with 'memory' you will tend to sing them with the accent on the wrong syllable of 'memory'

Take time over rhyme If you are going to use rhyme take time over it. Use a Rhyming dictionary or a Thesaurus to help you to find the right word.

Aim to surprise Don't make it obvious from the beginning of the line what word you will use as a rhyme

ALTERNATIVES TO RHYME

You may choose not to rhyme at all especially if your songs are going to be translated into other languages. However, if you are not going to use rhyme at all, or very little, you need to have a strong rhythmic feeling to your lyrics to make up for it. Below are some suggestions of what you could do in addition to rhyme or instead of using exact or near rhyme.

Use repeated phrases

Exact repetition of phrases can serve some of the purpose of rhyme both rhythmically and in ease of memorising.

e.g. 'What A Beautiful Name' (Ben Fielding & Brooke Ligertwood). The changing choruses start with the first line being repeated and then repeated again in the 4th and 6th lines reinforcing the message.

e.g. 'I Surrender' (Matt Crocker) Each verse ends with a repeated line.

Repetition of a phrase with a subtle change can also help when rhyme is not being used.

e.g. 'Jesus I believe in you/Jesus I belong to you' 'With All I Am' (Reuben Morgan)

e.g. 'So have Your way/Lord have Your way' Verse 3. 'Let There Be Light' (Matthew Crocker, Joel Houston, Michael Guy Chislett, Brooke Ligertwood, Scott Ligertwood, Jonas Myrin) In addition in this song there are phrases in the verses (e.g. 'God almighty/God of mercy' in v.1) that are repeated but reversed later. These serve as sound links

Use parallel constructions

This can take the form of a 4 or 5 exact rhyme that is expressed in a phrase and can be satisfying to the ear. It can also take the form of repeated parts of phrases that build on one another through to a conclusion.

e.g. 'And I'll live **what I** sing/**What I** say/**What I**'m learning every day.' from 'Forever And A Day' (Raymond Badham)

Use alliteration

Using two or more words in a line that start with the same sound can be effective and memorable although you need to be careful not to overdo it. 'Heavenly hosts hymn happy hallelujahs' is definitely overdoing it! The other problem is that it will definitely not translate so it is a mistake to rely on it too heavily. In the following examples alliteration is used sparingly but effectively.

e.g. '**Wh**om **h**ave I in **h**eaven but You' from 'Made Me Glad' (Miriam Webster)

e.g. 'You **m**et **m**e at the sinners' table/I found You **w**aiting by the **w**ell' from 'Shadow Step' (Joel Houston, Michael Guy Chislett)

Use parallel word endings

Because the words end in the same way they are not rhymes but the parallels are still helpful to the ear.

e.g. darkness/blindness; weakness/kindness from 'Sing (Your Love)' (Reuben Morgan) These words occur at the end of the lines.

'weakness/greatness' from 'Heart Like Heaven' (Matt Crocker, Joel Houston)

Use parallelism

A fundamental characteristic of Hebrew poetry is the way it tends to echo one thought with another not just as an exact repetition but taking the thought further. This extremely useful and attractive poetic device was used throughout the Psalms and elsewhere in the Bible. The connection between two or more poetic lines is found in the meaning rather than the sound link and this obviously has implications for translation as sense is much easier to translate than sound. Because this is quite a complex aspect of Hebrew poetry I have written a chapter on it at the end of the book in Appendix B for those who are interested in studying it further. Quite apart from being a useful tool for us as songwriters it also gives us an important insight into how Hebrew poetry works.

e.g. 'You have no rival/You have no equal' from 'What A Beautiful Name' (Ben Fielding & Brooke Ligertwood) The statement that God has no rival is taken further by making it clear that no one is His equal.

e.g. 'God is with us/God is on our side' from 'God Is Able' (Ben Fielding, Reuben Morgan, Arrangement Michael Guy Chislett). The truth that God is with us is developed further by the fact that it means that He is on our side.

SUMMARY

Rhyme sticks in the memory and so is a very useful tool to use.

Questions about rhyme.
What is it? Why use it? When do we rhyme? Which words do we rhyme? What is an identity? What is a rhyme scheme? What is near rhyme?

Techniques of rhyme.
Understand exact rhyme and near rhyme and how to use it.

Problem solving with rhyme.
Discover what traps to avoid and how to improve your technique.

Alternatives to rhyme.
These include repeated phrases, parallel constructions, alliteration, parallel word endings and parallelism.

EXERCISES

1. Exact rhyme
Go back to the lyrics that you wrote in Exercise 4 in Chapter 9 and rewrite them so that they contain at least one example of exact rhyme.

2. Near rhyme
- Find as many examples of assonance (echoed vowels) as you can for the following words: love, heart, mind, chain.

- Now find an example of consonance, para rhyme and augmented rhyme for each of them.

3. Alternatives to rhyme

Write another section, either verse or chorus, to the lyrics in Exercise 1 and use one of the alternatives to rhyme that I have suggested.

WORKING WITH A STRUCTURE

'Oceans' (Matt Crocker, Joel Houston, Salomon Ligthelm)

'All we had was a verse melody, but there was something about it that seemed to cling to us. It wasn't until we were in New York a few months later that we actually started working properly on the song. We found a chorus that we liked enough to put in the demo of the song, but we still felt that it needed a bridge. At this point lyrically we had nothing of weight besides the word 'Oceans' which was sung off the cuff over the demo...

Over the next two months we were trying to finish so many other songs that we kind of shelved the song. Not completely, but just to put it on hold till we knew what to do with it.

I decided to meet up with Salomon Ligthelm to try write some lyrics as we were rapidly losing time to finish the songs...All I could give him was the word 'oceans'. Joel and I had talked about the word as something to use as a focus of the song. Salomon came back to us with the thought of Peter stepping out of the boat and walking on water. The need to trust Jesus and step out into the unknown. This clicked with us straight away. Finally we had a direction for the song that made sense...

This was the first song we started out writing for the album [Empires] and it was the last song we finished...

We [Joel and Matt] took a look over all the ideas we already had and started piecing sentence together, line by line. It almost felt effortless to finish this song, which is so the opposite of how this song was to actually write. It always helps to have a strong theme to write around with clear direction. It makes finding lyrics so much easier.'

Matt Crocker

'I think of song structure as the ebb and flow of the song counterbalanced with the momentum of the song. A song that does this will have a good energy right through the song.'

Raymond Badham

'You don't have to conform to ONE specific structure every time. But then, in saying that, certain structures work well. It's all about playing within the boundaries.'

Marty Sampson

CHAPTER 12

THE IMPORTANCE OF STRUCTURE

I magine having breakfast at a little coffee shop by the beach. The sun is shining, the eggs and bacon are cooked to perfection and everything is well with the world until you order your first, much-needed coffee of the day. It's not that the waitress can't make a good cup of coffee. In fact she is an expert in the art of making filter coffee. The problem arises when she brings the coffee pot across and simply pours the coffee straight onto the table.

After the initial shock and liberal use of paper towels to mop everything up you ask her why she did it. She replies that she felt that the coffee needed to be free to find its own level. That it should express itself without the restrictions of a cup! The trouble is that coffee poured onto the table is useless to us. It does not serve the function for which it was intended. We need the cup to contain it so that we can enjoy it.

Structure, in the same way, holds everything together. Structure or form is to a song what a cup is to coffee. Just as the empty cup is the context and the coffee is the content, so in a song the structure holds the content in place. And in the same way that coffee spilling all over the table fails to satisfy the would-be drinker so a song without any structure also fails to satisfy the listener although they might not be able to say why that is quite as easily as our dripping coffee drinker can!

In this chapter we will look at some of the keys to good structure before moving on in to look at different song structures that have been used over the years and been found to work and some that are not so commonly used in worship writing and spending a whole chapter on Verse/Chorus form which is the most popular one. You may come up with something completely different again but you will still need to fulfil the basics of balance and design for your structure to satisfy the listener.

KEYS TO GOOD SONG STRUCTURE

I have labelled the different sections of a song with a letter so that, with each new musical section, the letter changes. Therefore a song which consists solely of repeated verses would be labelled AAA but a song with more contrast may be labelled ABAC which would mean that the first section of music is repeated after a contrasting section and that the song ends with a new section. The exception to this is Verse/Chorus form and here I will refer to Verse, Chorus, Bridge etc. since they are the terms that are most familiar.

Good structure involves repetition, contrast and development

In writing our songs we need to ensure that the artistic principles of repetition, contrast and development are present. When we listen to a song we want to hear repetition, especially of the main hook, but we also want some contrast. A song that simply repeats one idea over and over again quickly loses its appeal. In addition to this we want to feel that the song is going somewhere and that means that there needs to be some development both musically and lyrically. A strong structure can help to achieve this because it will contain within it all these elements.

If a song is simply a series of unconnected musical ideas following one after the other the listeners will be both confused and frustrated since there are no clear points of familiarity to come back to. This not only makes the song harder for them to learn, if it is intended for congregational worship, but they will be less likely to go away with a fragment of the song in their mind that will make them want to hear or sing it again.

This is equally true of lyric structure, as we have already discussed. If the lyrics lack a structure that includes repetition, contrast and development then the song will not work well. A common trap that novice songwriters can fall into is trying to say all that they know about their faith in one song rather than taking a concept and developing it.

Structure can be internal as well as external

Generally when we speak of song structure we are referring to the song in its entirety. As you plan your song you will most likely work with a Verse/Chorus structure. However structure also applies to a section within the song. In fact, understanding that a verse or chorus can have a structure as well as the song as a whole can help you with both lyrics and melody as you work within that mini framework. Some of the classic song structures such as AABA (e.g. Yesterday – Lennon/McCartney); ABAB (e.g. Moon River-Mercer) and ABAC (e.g. 'Prima Donna' – Lloyd Webber/Hart from 'Phantom of the Opera') may not lend themselves to the structure of a worship song as a whole but can be used for the internal melodic or lyric structure in a verse, chorus or bridge because they follow the principles of repetition and variation. Using the same labelling system for internal structure within a section as we have for the whole song we can see some different examples.

e.g. 'Just Let Me Say' (Geoff Bullock)   Each verse is in AABA form.

e.g. 'O Praise The Name (Anástasis)' (Marty Sampson, Benjamin Hastings, Dean Usher). The chorus is ABAB.

e.g. 'What A Beautiful Name' (Ben Fielding & Brooke Ligertwood) The verse is ABAB with a slight change at the end of the 2nd B to lead into the chorus.

e.g. 'Transfiguration' (Brooke Ligertwood, Scott Ligertwood, Aodhan King, Taya Smith) The verse is ABAB

e.g. 'Alive' (Aodhan King, Alexander Pappas) The chorus is ABAB

e.g. 'Sing (Your Love)' (Reuben Morgan) The verse is ABAC.

e.g. 'Ever Living God' (Raymond Badham) The verse is ABAC.

e.g. 'Cornerstone' (Jonas Myrin, Eric Liljero, Reuben Morgan) The verse is ABAC

Obviously there are many other variations on the internal structure of a section that could be used as well including simply building from line to line without any repetition. What also adds interest and variation is that the verse, chorus and bridge can all have different internal structures.

e.g. 'O Praise The Name (Anástasis)' (Marty Sampson, Benjamin Hastings, Dean Usher). The verse builds through from line to line without repetition ABCD but the chorus is ABAB.

Introduce variation on the repeats

We need to pay attention to the repeats in our songs whether they are in the internal or external structure. If a section is repeated a number of times then it is important to vary some of the details within that section. If there are a number of verses we may change the number of unstressed syllables or make little melodic changes or even add something.

e.g. 'Take All Of Me' (Marty Sampson) Notice the variation between verses 1 and 2 in terms of unstressed syllables. Notice also the little melodic changes between the verses especially at the end.

Sometimes the songwriter may only repeat part of a section. This can work well because it fulfils the principles of repetition and development at the same time.

e.g. 'Oceans' (Matt Crocker, Joel Houston, Salomon Ligthelm). The final chorus leaves out the 3rd line 'When oceans rise' which has the effect of the same melodic line being repeated three times before the final line. This clarifies that the song is ending.

e.g. 'Cornerstone' (Jonas Myrin, Eric Liljero, Reuben Morgan) In verse 2 the final line 'My anchor holds within the veil' is repeated an octave higher but this does not happen in verses 1 and 3.

Check the transitions

Problems can arise when we try to join two sections that are too different from one another. Even with the principle of contrast there needs to be a sense that each section develops or grows naturally out of the one before. Sometimes this means bringing elements of melody, harmony or lyrics into another section in a subtly changed form. At other times it simply means that we need to think a little harder about how we link the two sections. Maybe it will require a little change to the end of one section or a couple of instrumental bars to give more preparation harmonically or rhythmically.

e.g. 'One Way' (Jonathon Douglass, Joel Houston) The internal structure of the verse is basically AABAAB but the final B section ends differently so that it leads into the chorus.

e.g. 'This I Believe (The Creed)' (Matt Crocker, Ben Fielding).

The verse is basically ABCABC in structure but the final C section takes the melody up so that it naturally leads into the melody of the chorus.

Experimenting with different song structures can lead to greater creativity

It is very easy to become stuck in a rut as far as song structure is concerned and only to write in the one that is familiar to you. Probably for most people that would be Verse/Chorus form. Experimenting with different song forms though can lead to new and exciting ways of writing a song and I have looked at a few later in this chapter.

The more complex your song form is the more carefully you need to use it when writing for worship. A very complicated form with a number of different sections can create problems when it comes to repeating the song as we tend to do in worship. The song leader may end up putting the song in the 'too hard' basket if it is not obvious which sections can be repeated.

Structure must not become a straitjacket

There is always a danger in a book like this of ending up writing songs almost like painting by numbers. Once again then I want to stress that song structure, like every other song writing technique, is a servant not a master and should always reinforce the message of the song. Good use of form will be unobtrusive because it will serve to reinforce the message of the song rather than to dominate or constrict it. There is always room to depart from a classic song structure if that is what the song needs. However it is a good discipline if you are not used to thinking about structure to practice writing a song in its simplest form before developing outside it.

'*A great form can only serve to help a song.*'
Reuben Morgan

ALTERNATIVE SONG FORMS

There are a few song forms here that may be interesting and helpful in writing for worship. I have included them to remind us that there is life outside the Verse/Chorus format and in order to challenge our thinking on what could be possible.

AAA form

This form consists of a series of verses with no bridge or chorus. Often the verses are only 16 bars long. There may be an instrumental interlude at some point.

Lyrics Often in this form the title either begins or ends each verse and the verses may end with a refrain. This is a one or two line statement which is repeated from verse to verse. Note that a refrain is not a chorus. It simply ends the verse and the melody is a continuation of what has gone before whereas a chorus introduces new musical ideas and is usually at least eight bars long. This form lends itself well to story-telling and so it is important to go on a journey with it. Be careful to have a clear progression of thought.

e.g. 'Silent Night' (Traditional)

e.g. 'Hark The Herald Angels Sing' (words by Charles Wesley, Music by Felix Mendelssohn). Notice the repeated refrain at the end of each verse.

Music A strong melody is essential as the music will be repeated a number of times. Try to develop a musical motif that the listener will enjoy hearing again. Follow the principle of putting the hook on the title or in the refrain. Start the verses strongly.

Use of this form in worship This form is good for any song where the focus is on the lyrics and so has been a popular form for hymn writing both past and present as it lends itself to developing a concept through a number of verses.

> e.g. 'Amazing Grace' (John Newton)
> e.g. 'When I Survey The Wondrous Cross' (Isaac Watts)
> e.g. 'Jesus What A Beautiful Name' (Tanya Riches)

Twelve bar blues

Basic structure Each verse is 12 bars long, hence the name, and is divided into three lyric lines with four bars in each. The lyrics do not usually fill the four bars but tend to leave one to one and a half bars free for instrumental or vocal fills.

Lyrics The theme is traditionally one of complaint which is not surprising since the history of the blues was rooted in the slave trade. However, in the Spiritual that grew out of the Blues, there is often a strong sense of Christian endurance and faith as well. The lyric form is a couplet stretched to three lines by repeating the first line. Later the blues developed so that there were three different lyric lines often using near rather than exact rhyme.

Music The blues scale is developed from the Pentatonic scale that forms the basis of much ethnic music. The traditional 'blue' notes are found by taking the major scale and flattening the 3rd and 7th notes by a semitone. For Jazz blues flatten the 5th as well. The tonality falls somewhere between the major and minor key.

The classic chord pattern of the blues is:

```
I   I   I   I7              C   C   C   C7
IV  IV  I   I        or     F   F   C   C
V   IV  I   V7              G   F   C   G7
```

The rhythms of the Blues are influenced by its African heritage and were the forerunners of rock music.

Use of this form in worship Spirituals would often base their lyrics on Bible stories. They would also frequently work on the concept of leader and response. Probably in contemporary worship the best use is in a fast moving song with a rock feel.

Free form or through composed

Structure In this form there is no set structure that repeats sections but simply a musical development from phrase to phrase. However even in the free form or through composed song where there is no clear repetition of sections there is repetition, contrast and development as the song is built on a series of variations that develop an original motif. The sense of unity comes from that development of lyric and motif.

e.g. 'You'll Never walk Alone' from 'Carousel' (Rodgers/ Hammerstein) In this song each bar develops from the one before and none are repeated.

This form works well in a song in which the composer wants to affect his audience deeply. The essence of the free form song is the way in which the composer uses variation technique to develop and change his original motif. This may be done melodically, harmonically or rhythmically. Lyric development and repetition is also important in the way in which the song gains a sense of unity despite the lack of obvious repeated sections

e.g. 'No More' from 'Into The Woods' (Stephen Sondheim)

Internal use of this form in worship Many worship songs use a free form in miniature when building through a verse or chorus.

Any song that does not have clearly repeated lines in its verse or chorus but builds through from line to line could be said to be free form to a degree.

e.g. 'To You Alone' (Reuben Morgan) In both the verse and chorus Reuben builds his melody on repeated sequences whether they are rising or falling and that along with the repeated 'every' in the verse and 'all' in the chorus creates variation and yet unity in the song. The external structure of the song though is a straightforward Verse/Chorus form.

External use of this form in worship This is a very risky form to use in worship but one place where it could possibly be used might be in an inspirational anthem that is only sung through once although it would be hard for a congregation to learn a whole song that has no repetition. Another way would be to use it in an extended song on an album where there is a lyric or melodic theme that is developed. Usually it would still contain repeated sections but perhaps move into more of a free form later in the song.

e.g. 'Water To Wine' (Joel Houston) This starts as a typical verse/chorus structure but then moves into a partial free form structure later with a repeated lyric and melodic hook on 'So I'll stay' which is introduced in the chorus and then continues in repeated sections that explore related lyrics in a much freer style.

SUMMARY

Structure is vital to a song because it holds everything together.

Keys to good song structure
Good structure involves repetition, contrast and development; structure can be internal as well as external; introduce variation on the repeats; check the transitions; experimenting with different

song structures can lead to greater creativity; structure must not become a strait jacket.

Alternative song forms

There are a variety of song forms but not all lend themselves easily to a worship song but some possibilities include AAA form, 12 Bar Blues and free form or through composed.

EXERCISES

1. Analysis of song forms

Choose three of your favourite worship songs and work out their structure.

Do they contain the principles of repetition, contrast and development? If so, how is that worked out?

How do the transitions between the sections work?

2. AAA form

- Write a song that is three verses long in this form.
- Include a refrain at the end of each verse.
- Make sure that you develop your thought from verse to verse.

3. Internal forms

- Write a melody that follows an ABAB structure. Allow four bars for each section.
- Write a melody that is in an AABA format.

CHAPTER 13

VERSE/CHORUS FORM

It is not surprising that this is by far the most common structure that is used in worship songs. It is a very strong form with the verses telling the story and contrasting, catchy choruses that contain the hook and germ theme of the song. Of course another reason that it so dominates other forms is that, because it is the one we hear the most, we naturally tend to imitate it.

Verse/chorus form has had an interesting history. In the early twentieth century, especially in Music Theatre, the verse used to be the part of a song that set the scene and preceded the melodic or catchy tune. It really served as an introduction and there would only generally be one verse. These verses became expendable until only the chorus section remained, often in AABA form, and that was what was sung or recorded when the song was removed from its original setting. Often the melody of the verse was fairly unmemorable.

When Rock music hit the scene the picture changed again in that the chorus was placed before the verse. Contemporary Verse/

Chorus form, as we know it now, developed when the verse was once again placed before the chorus but was no longer expendable as it had been originally. The verse led the listener to the hook, which was in the chorus.

'The verse chorus structure is a simple, appealing, easy to sing style, and very common…It's all about packaging your melodies well…If you are sending a package somewhere, you use a cardboard box because it's cheap, easy to use, accessible for others and extremely functional.' **Marty Sampson**

THE BASIC ELEMENTS OF THE VERSE/CHORUS SONG

The Verse/Chorus song contains some clear elements with some optional extras to add to the interest and also the development of the song.

The verse

The verse gives the information that explains the reason for the message of the chorus. Any new information comes in the verses. It is important to make sure that you leave yourself somewhere to go in the chorus so don't make your verses so dramatic musically and lyrically that your chorus ends up as an anticlimax. Go on an emotional journey in your lyrics and if you have two or more verses in your song make sure that they progress lyrically.

e.g. 'Mighty To Save' (Reuben Morgan, Ben Fielding) Verse 1 looks at our need for a Saviour and then verse 2 describes our response to salvation.

e.g. 'Not Today' (Joel Houston, Matt Crocker). Verse 1 looks at our faith response to trouble and verse 2 looks at the basis for the confidence as it asks questions of how the enemy reacted when Jesus died and rose again.

e.g. 'Man Of Sorrows' (Matt Crocker, Brooke Ligertwood). Verse 1 speaks of Jesus' betrayal; verse 2 speaks of Jesus' trial and crucifixion; verse 3 speaks of the redemptive purpose of Jesus' death and verse 4 speaks of the resurrection.

e.g. 'Behold (Then Sings My Soul)' (Joel Houston) Verse 1 speaks of the Father, verse 2 of the Son and verse 3 of the Holy Spirit.

The chorus

The chorus usually has a lyric, melodic, instrumental or rhythmic hook to make it memorable. This may be very simple and will generally, although not always, be based around the title of the song. What the chorus must contain is the song's central message.

e.g. 'My Redeemer Lives' (Reuben Morgan) In this chorus the title is repeated four times and that is it. There is no doubt about what the message of the song is!

e.g. 'O Praise the Name (Anástasis)' (Marty Sampson, Benjamin Hastings, Dean Ussher). The chorus is slightly more involved than the previous two but still very focused in its message

e.g. 'Calvary' (Reuben Morgan, Jonas Myrin, Mrs. Walter G. Taylor) The key phrase is 'Calvary covers it all' and that appears in every part of the song.

Other choruses can be far more complex and developed. The important thing here is not to try to say too much and lose sight of the central message.

e.g. 'No Other Name' (Jonas Myrin, Joel Houston) The chorus is long (10 lines) but 4 of those lines repeat the title of the song 'No other Name' and so the central message is clear.

The bridge

The bridge is often shorter than the chorus and normally comes between the final chorus and its repeat, although there are exceptions to this. It allows for more contrast and development than verse/chorus alone. A standard format looks like this:

Verse/Chorus/Verse/Chorus/Bridge/Chorus

The purpose of the bridge is to add new lyric and musical material to the song. It is important to make sure that the words being added complement the message rather than taking the song in a completely new direction.

e.g. 'More Than Life' (Reuben Morgan) Here the bridge adds to the song by focusing on the cross and asking questions rather than making statements.

e.g. 'Man Of Sorrows' (Matt Crocker, Brooke Ligertwood) The bridge contains a confession of faith in what Jesus' death has accomplished with a simple, repetitive melody that is easy to pick up.

e.g. 'Oceans' (Matt Crocker, Joel Houston, Salmon Ligthelm) The focus of the bridge takes us further lyrically in that it becomes a response to God's call to trust Him.

Make sure that your hook lyrically and musically is in the chorus not the bridge so that the bridge does not compete with the chorus. There have been a number of occasions when what a student has labeled the bridge is really the chorus in terms of its musical and lyric significance. I have to admit to doing it myself when I co-wrote a song with a student and started with the bridge idea. Nothing else in the song ever matched up to that original idea and yet it wasn't suitable as the chorus because the lyrics did not carry the heart of the song.

e.g. 'Elohim' (Marty Sampson) Although the whole song is lovely it is the bridge that has leant itself most to worship and we often sing the bridge on its own as part of the worship set.

The pre-chorus

The pre-chorus section grows out of the verse and adds tension as the listener awaits the chorus. It is often just a couplet although it can be longer. It is also known as a climb which makes sense as it generally bridges the gap between the pitch of the verse and that of the chorus.

Verse/PreChorus/Chorus/Verse/PreChorus/Chorus/Bridge/Chorus

e.g. 'Need You Here' (Reuben Morgan) The pre-chorus lyrics are: 'I only want to be where you are' and by the end we have climbed an octave to the pitch of the chorus.

e.g. 'Your Word' (Chris Davenport). The pre-chorus 'The lamp unto my feet/The light unto my path' expresses how the word works in our lives and leads into the confession of the chorus.

e.g. 'Passion' (Bede Benjamin-Korporaal, Ben Tan, Laura Toggs, Aodhan King). The pre-chorus 'I know you love me so' is a response to what Jesus has done for us.

The Outro or Tag

Often in worship songs an outro or tag may be used at the end of the song. It is usually very simple and easy to sing and serves to extend the moment of worship. Because of its simplicity the congregation does not need to concentrate on technicalities but can simply use the words as a basis from which to move into free worship.

e.g. 'I will worship' ('With All I Am' – Reuben Morgan) These words pick up from the bridge but lead out of the song into free worship.

e.g. 'Prince Of Peace' (Joel Houston, Matt Crocker, Dylan Thomas) The tag picks up on elements of the 2nd bridge that can be repeated and potentially lead into free worship.

'I remember that I used to sit on buses and just work on song writing. I would work through the melodies and think of a song in my head that I knew was a good song. I would just analyse music in my head. I would think through the melody and the chords and how the verse was and then how the chorus lifted. I would think about how the chorus worked in the structure of the song and I'd try and write paralleling all of the concepts and all of the principles in my head, just trying to get the rudiments of it, the craft of it. I'm real glad of those long bus experiences.' **Reuben Morgan**

VARIATIONS ON THE STANDARD VERSE/CHORUS FORM

Once you have mastered the basic form then it is time to experiment with variations on it. Here are a few suggestions but there are many other variations that you could try. Notice that all of them fulfil the principle of repetition, variation and development.

Postponing the chorus

You may choose to postpone the chorus so that the congregation sings two verses instead of one before reaching it. This will probably mean that your second verse will finish slightly differently musically to the first as they are moving to different musical sections.

e.g. 'No Other Name' (Jonas Myrin, Joel Houston) The chorus is sung after the 2nd verse

e.g. 'Alive' (Aodhan King, Alexander Pappas) The chorus is sung after the 2nd verse

e.g. 'I Surrender' (Matt Crocker). In this song all 4 verses are sung before the chorus is sung for the first time. However at the end of verse 2 Matt adds a line 'I surrender' that is not found in any of the other 3 verses and this serves to anticipate the chorus.

Pre-empting the chorus

This can be risky as it can take away from the effect of the chorus but if you are wanting to strongly emphasise a thought it can work well as it does in the example below.

e.g. 'Calvary' (Reuben Morgan, Jonas Myrin, Mrs Walter G. Taylor) The melodic and lyric hook 'Calvary covers it all' is sung at the end of the verse and the end of the chorus.

Ending the song with a final verse

This can be effective in introducing a final, often reflective, thought that you want to leave the congregation reflecting on rather than the emotional high of the chorus

e.g. 'Let There Be Light' (Matthew Crocker, Joel Houston, Michael Guy Chislett, Brooke Ligertwood, Scott Ligertwood, Jonas Myrin) Verse 3 – 'Let the light that shines above/Become the light that shines in us/There's no darkness in Your way/So have your way/Lord have your way.' These lines pick up on the start of the song but now present the congregation with a personal challenge to surrender to God.

Ending the song with a more extended outro/tag

Generally the tag is very simple and grows out of the chorus or bridge but it could be more extended.

e.g. 'Behold (Then Sings My Soul)' (Joel Houston). The outro introduces new music and brings a satisfying conclusion to the prayer in the 3rd verse as it looks forward to the day when the work on earth is done and ends 'Behold the Lord our God will lead us home'. Notice that in the outro although it is a new section it includes both 'Then sings my soul' and 'Behold' which ties it back to the rest of the song.

Multiple choruses

This allows for the verses to go on a journey that take them beyond the lyrics of the original chorus. Although it can work in a song for general worship it is also suitable for a longer song that may be intended for an album or an item in a service.

e.g. 'What A Beautiful Name' (Ben Fielding & Brooke Ligertwood). In this song the chorus changes each time with the description of the Name of Jesus moving from 'beautiful' to 'wonderful' and finally 'powerful'. 'Beautiful' relates to the first verse that speaks of the glory of creation revealed in Christ; 'wonderful' relates to the wonder of salvation described in the 2nd verse and 'powerful' follows the bridge which speaks of the victory and sovereignty of God.

e.g. 'So Will I (100 Billion Times)' (Joel Houston, Benjamin Hastings, Michael Fatkin). This is even more complex but each new chorus relates to the verse that precedes it. Verse 1 speaks of creation and chorus 1 tells of the praises of creation ending 'If creation sings Your praises so will I'. Verse 2 speaks of God's word and its power and chorus 2 addresses the continuing obedience of creation to God's word ending 'If creation still obeys You so will I'. The bridge takes the hook of the chorus but then develops it in a free style while the lyrics continue the theme of praising as creation does. Verse 3 refers to salvation and chorus 3 speaks of the effects of Christ's surrender and ends 'If You gladly chose surrender so will I'. Then there is then an extended section of chorus 3 which moves from speaking about 100 billion to 8 billion and relates to Christ's love for humanity ending 'If You gave Your life to love them so will I'. The song ends with a tag and a powerful final line 'You're the One who never leaves the one behind' bringing the whole idea of 100 billion down to the one. Although the structure of this song appears to be very complex, the repeated themes actually make it very easy to pick up.

Multiple bridges.

Again this may work in terms of the journey of the song and at times may be used as an extended final section of worship. The key is to keep the focus of the song and not make the bridge too complex musically.

e.g. 'Prince Of Peace' (Joel Houston, Matt Crocker, Dylan Thomas). After the two verses and chorus the song goes into bridge 1 which is an almost warlike confession of faith in the face of trouble and then moves into bridge 2 which is a more reflective address to the singer's heart to be still. Both bridges are very simple musically but contrasting in mood.

e.g. 'Open Heaven (River Wild) (Matt Crocker, Marty Sampson) This has two distinct bridges that express a longing for more of the Holy Spirit and lend themselves to repetition before returning to the final chorus.

SUMMARY

The elements of the Verse/Chorus song include:

The verse.
The verse gives the information that leads into the message of the chorus.

The chorus.
The chorus contains the memorable hook and central message of the song.

The bridge.
The bridge adds new lyric and musical material to add contrast and development.

The pre-chorus.
The pre-chorus adds tension by delaying the chorus.

The outro or tag.
The outro or tag is generally very simple and serves to extend the moment of worship.

Variations on the verse chorus form.
There are a number of variations to try once you have mastered the basic form.

EXERCISES

1. Verse and chorus

Write a new verse and chorus or rework one that you have written in previous exercises applying what you have learned in this chapter where necessary.

2. Add a bridge

- Look at what you have lyrically so far and consider whether there is something else that you could usefully say in the song that will add another dimension to the message without taking you somewhere completely different.
- Think about what you could do musically that would bring some contrast to what we have heard before. Make sure that you do not write something that is more memorable than the chorus.

3. Include a prechorus

This may involve rethinking your lyrics and melody on the verse so that you can lead into it. Don't try to do too much in it.

SECTION 5

WRITING THE MUSIC

On 'Shout To The Lord' (Darlene Zschech)

'Shout to the Lord' was never really written as in pondered over. It was more of a cry, a prayer and I just started singing this song. It probably took 20 minutes all up to complete. I never even sang it to anyone for a while, as I was so unsure that it was a valid song.'

Darlene Zschech

On 'O Praise the Name (Anástasis)'
(Marty Sampson, Benjamin Hastings, Dean Ussher)

'We crafted the melody almost line by line, and tried to pay attention to the nuances of what the melody was doing as a whole once the lines were placed together as one stanza. We looked at the clock after what seemed like only minutes, and our time was up for the day. It took a few more months of back and forward from that day to finish the song as it is now.' [20]

Marty Sampson

---

20 Adapted Marty Sampson *'Song Story: O Praise The Name (Anastasis)'* 6/10/2015. Used with permission https://hillsong.com/collected/blog/2015/10/song-story-o-praise-the-name-anastasis/#.WVSiFliGOM8

On 'Man Of Sorrows' (Matt Crocker & Brooke Ligertwood)

'One afternoon my dear friend Matt Crocker showed me a verse melody idea he had, which I immediately loved. It had a hymn-like meter, yet within its classic movement there seemed infinite possibility to be able to really tell a great story with the lyric. We read Isaiah 53 together...The phrase 'man of sorrows' jumped out at us and we knew we had our first line and title. From the simple but poetic biblical phrase anchoring the verse from the first line, we were able to really dig into the story of the Saviour from Pilate to the crucifixion...What I appreciate about this song is the narrative verses, declarative chorus and then the bridge that is a deeply personal response and victory cry for all that has been sung before it'

Brooke Ligertwood

'What can be more powerful than music to raise the spirits of the sad, to frighten the happy, to make the despondent valiant, to calm those who are enraged, to reconcile those filled with hatred...?' [21]

Martin Luther

21 Richard Viladesau *Theology and the Arts* Paulist Press USA 2000 p.25

CHAPTER 14

WRITING MELODIES

'Yesterday' (Lennon/McCartney), 'Ave Maria' (Gounod), 'Silent Night' (Gruber), 'Memory' (Lloyd Webber), and 'Autumn Leaves' (Kosma/Provert/Mercer), have all been phenomenally successful songs. Obviously the lyrics are important but many of these songs have been recorded and re-recorded simply as instrumentals. So what is it about these songs that has captured people's hearts?

I believe that the key to their success is that they all have a strong, catchy, well-constructed melody that you want to hear again and again. The message seems to be that, if you want your song to last, you need to write a strong melody. That is why ballads tend to be recorded more often and last longer than songs which are based purely on whatever rhythm is in fashion at the moment. Rhythms can quickly sound dated and harmony, however intricate, is not enough on its own to sustain a song. Even a brilliant arrangement can only disguise a weak melody temporarily.

As writers of worship songs we must never compromise on the message of the song but if we can match our lyrics to great melodies then our songs will last longer and have greater impact. Let us look at some of the elements that make a strong melody.

A STRONG MELODY SHOULD BE:

A melody that is worth repeating This is very important, especially in slower songs and especially because worship songs tend to be repeated a few times. Will your melody stand repeating or does it become boring? Is there something about it that catches the interest?

- **A melody that has a strong structure** Find a motif and develop it. Do not plagiarize. Work for a sense of balance in your melody and a structure that complements the direction of your words.
- **A melody that touches the emotions** Write melodies that create emotional responses and that linger in the listener's mind.
- **A melody that the congregation can sing** Make sure that your melody has a vocal range and structure that can be sung by an inexperienced singer.
- **A melody that compliments the words** The melody should enhance the message of the song rather than conflict with it.

'We often sing the same songs in our churches for years. So we need to try to write interesting and robust melodies that can stand up to years of road-testing.' **Ben Fielding**

PRACTICAL STEPS TO BUILDING A STRONG MELODY:

There are a number of techniques that help to build a strong melody and it is worth understanding and practicing them all.

Find the melodic 'hook'

A hook is the most memorable part of a melody. A hook or motif is what stays in the listener's mind when everything else has gone. It may only involve two or three different notes but they have been put together in a distinctive and memorable way. The melodic hook is associated with the most important words of the song which will tend to occur in the chorus of most worship songs unless another song structure is used. Because of this the title of your song will often provide inspiration for a hook that will help to convey its message in its emotional impact.

e.g. 'Shout To The Lord' (Darlene Zschech) 2 pitch hook on 'Shout to the Lord'

e.g. 'One Way' (Jonathon Douglass, Joel Houston) A rising 2 pitch hook on 'One way'

e.g, 'Heart Like Heaven' (Matt Crocker, Joel Houston) A falling 2 pitch hook on 'Heart like heaven'

e.g. 'Worthy Is The Lamb' (Darlene Zschech) A 3 pitch hook on 'Worthy is the Lamb'

e.g. 'Mighty To Save' (Reuben Morgan, Ben Fielding) A 3 pitch hook on 'Mighty to Save'

e.g. 'Let There Be Light' (Matthew Crocker, Joel Houston, Michael Guy Chislett, Brooke Ligertwood, Scott Ligertwood, Jonas Myrin) A rising 2 pitch hook on 'Let there be light'

Experiment with different intervals If you find that all your hooks sound the same, then experiment. It may be that you have become stuck with using certain intervals. Try unusual combinations and discover how different intervals can create different moods. e.g. rising minor 7th (e.g. C-Bb) 'There's a place for us' (Bernstein /Sondheim from West Side Story); rising major 2nd (e.g. C-D) 'People' (Styne/Merrill); rising octave (e.g. C-C) 'Bring him home' (Les Miserables – Boulbil/Schonberg); descending major 3rd (e.g. E-C) 'Summertime' (Porgy and Bess – Gershwin)

e.g. 'Water Into Wine' (Joel Houston). The 2 pitch hook on 'So I'll stay' in the chorus is based around a rising major 6th that catches our attention and emphasises the word 'stay'.

e.g. 'I Surrender' (Matt Crocker). The 2 pitch hook on 'I'll surrender' is a falling minor 2nd from the 6th to the 5th.

Revise your hook if necessary Since there are only 12 possible pitches to work with it is easy to come up with a hook that sounds the same as that in another composer's song. That does not mean that you necessarily have to reject your hook completely but you will need to rearrange it and then develop it in a new and interesting way so that you do not plagiarise

e.g. The chorus to 'What A Beautiful Name' (Ben Fielding & Brooke Ligertwood) is very simple and memorable and we sang it many times in 2016. It was not surprising then that a new song that was written (that shall remain nameless!) inadvertently used that hook almost exactly in its chorus including the descending sequence. This song was too good to throw away so the songwriters tweaked the chorus so that it was sufficiently different to be original.

Build the melody phrase by phrase

Balance your phrases Melodic development is all to do with balance. As a rule a writer will develop his hook into a two bar phrase and balance that with another one and build from there. Even when a writer deliberately breaks from the 2+2 pattern there should still be an internal balance in the construction of the melody that satisfies the ear.

e.g. 'Majesty' (Stu Garrard and Martin Smith). Listen to the chorus of this song and see how beautifully the phrases are balanced.

e.g. 'Broken Vessels (Amazing Grace)' (Joel Houston, Jonas Myrin) In the verse we have four two bar phrases that build through the verse. Notice also how the first two bar phrases rise and fall within the phrase 'All those pieces/Broken and scattered'

Think in terms of question and answer It helps to think of these two bar phrases in terms of question and answer. If the melodic line of the first two bars rises then the melodic line of the next two should fall. The fall may be delayed by the use of sequence or repetition but eventually it needs to happen.

e.g. 'Captain' (Benjamin Hastings, Seth Simmons) The verse structure is built on question and answer phrases that balance each other beautifully.

e.g. 'Your Word' (Chris Davenport) The verse is built on question and answer phrases that build through the verse.

e.g. 'Water To Wine' (Joel Houston) The chorus is built on rising and falling phrases

Develop your phrases into a section Once you have developed a four bar phrase then you can expand it into a section. This is usually done by adding another 4 bar phrase. You follow the same principles of balance but may also aim to take the emotional impact of the melody further.

There are no hard and fast rules. If the song needs it you can build 5, 7, or 9 bar phrases or any other combination. The principle of balance is what is important. Does it work musically? e.g. 'Yesterday' (Lennon/McCartney) was built on 7 bar verses.

Furtwangler 'understood that music is not about statements or about being. It's about becoming. It's not the statement of a phrase that is really important, but how you get there and how you leave it and how you make the transition to the next phrase.' Daniel Barenboim[22]

e.g. 'Shout To The Lord' (Darlene Zschech) One of the reasons that this song has been so successful is because of the beautifully constructed melody with its balanced phrases that build through to the chorus.

e.g. 'No Other Name' (Jonas Myrin, Joel Houston) The verse builds through four 4 bar phrases with lots of space in them. The first two phrases are repeated and then the third phrase rises in pitch and contains more lyrics moving directly into the final phrase 'The greatest One of all'. This has the effect of driving the verse forward.

'While melodies and cadences can be familiar sometimes a creative melody can make a word like 'Hallelujah' sing like it has never been sung before' **Ben Fielding**

IDEAS ON HOW TO DEVELOP YOUR MELODY

Here are some suggestions for developing your melody if you are feeling blocked.

Start with a chord progression

Often a chord progression can spark off a melody especially if you have put some interesting chords together. The danger is that you

22 Daniel Barenboim and Edward W.Said *Parallels and Paradoxes* Bloomsbuy Publishing PLC UK 2002 p.21

can tie your melody too closely to the chords so that when it is sung unaccompanied it sounds weak because it does not have a strongly developed shape in its own right.

Start with a rhythm pattern

This can often inspire strong melodies especially if you decide to work simply with the rhythm and add the chords later. You are then freed from the constraints of trying to fit your melody around certain notes but you have the rhythmic framework already worked out.

Find different ways to develop your hook

Work with ideas such as changing the chords underneath the hook; changing the intervals slightly or simply repeating part of the hook.

'Melody for me is the heart of a song. I spend countless hours during the day and awake at night teasing out melodies, trying to find the best and moulding sections and lyric ideas together. Most of it is trial and error. It's a mystery where the real great melodies come from because they are almost always unexpected and unforced but they all need sculpting.'
Reuben Morgan

Experiment with sequences

This involves repeating a phrase at either a progressively higher or lower pitch two or more times with careful adjustments to the intervals so that you do not change key each time! This is a useful device for building a melody from an original motif and the secret lies in not overdoing it. Generally three repetitions are enough.

e.g. 'You Are Worthy' (Darlene Zschech) The verse repeats the melody on the first two lines with a small addition at the end of the second line but then, on the third line the melody is repeated a tone higher which has the effect of lifting the whole energy of the song while still basically using the same melody.

e.g. 'To You Alone' (Reuben Morgan) The melody of the first line of the verse is repeated in the third line but a tone lower and without adjustments to keep it in the same key which makes for some very interesting harmonies.

e.g. 'Broken Vessels (Amazing Grace)' (Joel Houston, Jonas Myrin). The chorus, using the well known words 'Amazing Grace,' is set to a new melody that is based on a rising sequence of three phrases repeated twice.

Try scale and arpeggio patterns

Often scales or parts of scales can form an interesting melodic pattern. e.g. 'Phantom of the Opera' (Lloyd Webber/Hart) uses a descending melodic minor scale; 'Habanera' from Bizet's opera 'Carmen' uses a descending chromatic scale; descending major scale but using leaps to give it interest; 'Over the Rainbow' from 'The Wizard of Oz' (Harburg/Arlen) is built around a descending major scale but uses leaps to give it interest.

e.g. 'What A Beautiful Name' (Ben Fielding, Brooke Ligertwood). The bridge 'Death could not hold You' is built around the D major triad.

Know when to write simple melodies

A very simple, repetitive melody can often work well especially if, at some point, there is a memorable contrasting section that it can explode into. An up tempo song does not need an elaborate melody since the interest is rhythmic rather than melodic.

e.g. 'Transfiguration' (Brooke Ligertwood, Scott Ligertwood, Aodhan King, Taya Smith) The verse melody is very simple and repetitive using only a limited range in patterns of 2+2 that serve as question and answer phrases. Then the chorus starts at a higher pitch and covers a wider range 'Holy is the Lord revealed' although still using question and answer phrases. The bridge section reverses the falling line of the chorus 'Now I know' and adds extra contrast.

Work on the climax of the song

The higher the key, the brighter the sound as singers then use their head rather than their chest register. Make sure that the climax of the song emotionally and lyrically coincides with the climax of the melodic line. That is where we find the highest, loudest and longest notes. In most songs it will usually occur in the chorus.

e.g. 'Your Word' (Chris Davenport) The chorus has the highest, longest notes in the song on 'Your Word will not be shaken etc.'

e.g. 'Mighty To Save' (Reuben Morgan, Ben Fielding) The verse is lower in pitch and uses a fairly narrow range of intervals in contrast to the chorus that builds through to the major hook of the song 'Mighty to save' which reaches the highest point melodically.

e.g. 'Christ Is Enough' (Reuben Morgan, Jonas Myrin) The chorus is the high point melodically of the song with the emphasis musically on the words 'Christ' and 'enough' which summarises the message of the song.

Include some contrast

A contrasting section can be achieved by changing the general pitch of the melody; by using smaller or larger intervals than previously; by using contrasting rhythm patterns and note values; by changing key or mode or in many other ways.

e.g. 'Oceans' (Matt Crocker, Joel Houston, Salomon Ligthelm). The verse is low in pitch and uses small intervals in building the melody but the chorus starts with a major 6th interval and the melody is general higher pitched and more open.

Add a surprise

Sometimes it is good to put something unexpected into the melody although we have to be careful not to overdo it or the song will be difficult to learn.

e.g. 'My Hope' (Darlene Zschech) The hook on the chorus catches our interest because Darlene has used a C natural instead of the C# that would be expected in the key of D major. 'My hope is in the **name** of the Lord.'

e.g. 'Not Today' (Joel Houston, Matt Crocker) The verse melody, although very simple, has a twist to it as the first half of the verse ends with a mini trill on 'more' and then the second half repeats exactly except for the end which drops down a third on 'heart' which makes the melody much more interesting.

'Melody is what people appropriate most. It's the take-home factor of the song. People won't walk out of church singing your chord progression, and they will remember your lyrics because they've remembered the melody. And the harmony is what colours the melody.' **Raymond Badham**

PROBLEMS TO AVOID

Recognising these danger areas can be a huge key to writing a strong melody.

Lack of direction

Always have a sense of direction when you construct a melody. Aim somewhere. Arrive there. Then move on somewhere else. Do not let two or more phrases settle on the same pitch or you will find that your melody is going nowhere and that you are continually being pulled back to the same chord. I have found this to be a common problem with novice songwriters. This is especially true when the verse or chorus is long because then the repetition is more noticeable.

e.g. 'Broken Vessels (Amazing Grace)' (Joel Houston, Jonas Myrin) I wrote earlier about the balance of the phrases in the verse of the song. The first two phrases repeat the melody and so settle on the same note but then the melody rises to a climax in the 3rd phrase on 'not forsaken' before resolving on 'set free'. However if Joel had simply repeated the first two phrases four times ending on the same note each time the melody would have had far less impact. Try singing the whole verse to the melody of the first two lines and you will see what I mean!

Lack of balance

Do not keep going in the same direction with your melody for very long, especially if you are using wide jumps. Apart from violating the principle of balance it can begin to sound a bit melodramatic as you continue higher and higher or lower and lower.

A difficult vocal range

Write what you can sing yourself unless you happen to be a professional singer! Worship songs generally need a range of less than an octave. Check what notes you are making your singer sing at the end of lines. Check the tessitura of your song. The tessitura is the pitch at which most of the song is sung. Too many notes at the top or the bottom of the vocal range become very tiring to sing.

Be aware of possible key changes for smaller groups. However a small group needs the songs to be pitched lower whereas a large congregation will cope with higher notes. Of course a small group could transpose a song that is written in too high a key but it may lack the personnel with the skills to do that. After all a song that has been written in F major and needs to be transposed down a semitone or tone suddenly moves from one flat in the key signature to either four sharps or three flats. A very different proposition for an inexperienced musician!

One of the challenges that we have found in on our team is that the men can sometimes write songs that are too high for the women to sing an octave up and too low for them if they sing in the male range. Conversely the women can sometimes write songs that are rather low for the men. This is because the typical contemporary voice tends to be alto for women and tenor for men. As a result there is often some compromising in terms of key but it is something to be aware of when writing for your particular voice. Think of the vocal ranges of the opposite sex when you are writing.

e.g. 'O Praise The Name' (Anástasis) (Marty Sampson, Benjamin Hastings, Dean Usher). This song is a great favourite but it does present a challenge. The chorus hits a top F which is definitely a stretch for the average congregation so they tend to drop down the octave and that loses some of the emotional impact of lifting into the chorus that was intended. I wonder how many churches have transposed this song into a lower key in order to avoid this challenge.

'I think it's a bad choice not to make a melody sing-able if you're trying to write for a congregation. If you're writing a song for a congregation then it needs to be in a good range for example and the intervals can't be too jumpy…One of my

goals with writing a melody for a church song is that the church would sound good singing it whether the song is being sung in a small group or whatever.' **Reuben Morgan**

A difficult melodic line

It is easy to write a melody that sounds great on a keyboard but which is very difficult to sing because of the intervals involved or the lengths of the phrases. The melodic line must be tied firmly to the harmonies that go underneath it if your congregation is going to be able to learn it quickly. Your congregation would also like to be able to take a breath occasionally!

I remember as a student in London being asked to sing a song written by a fellow student who was a piano major. She had basically written for piano rather than voice and that led to some very tricky phrases ending on impossibly high notes and unsingable words.

e.g. 'Elohim' (Marty Sampson). The verse melody is not immediately accessible to a congregation with its unusual melodic shape. However because it is clearly tied to the harmonies it makes it easier to learn. The chorus and bridge are both much simpler melodies which adds contrast.

A confusing message

Avoid writing a melody that does not serve to communicate the message of the song. A beautiful melody that cuts across the sense of the lyrics is poor prosody.

A writing-by-numbers approach

Although there are a number of elements in melody writing that can help you to improve your skills they must always be viewed as tools rather than rules. Ultimately a melody works or does not work according to its basic musicality and emotions even if it ignores some of the techniques outlined here.

'There are ways of writing melodies in a formulaic way. But for myself, I always try to put myself into a moment spiritually and emotionally and just start singing out. It can be one of the most vulnerable things you will ever do, especially when co-writing, but I think every songwriter has to face the moment where they decide if they are willing to become vulnerable in front of others or not. Once you have the general idea of the melody, then you can take some of those formulas you have for melodies and then apply them to the melody you have.'
Matt Crocker

SUMMARY

Strong melodies are one of the keys to writing a song that lasts. Such melodies should be worth repeating; have a strong structure; touch the emotions; be singable for a congregation and compliment the words.

Practical steps to building a strong melody include:

Finding the melodic 'hook'
The hook is the most memorable part of the melody and needs careful work.

Building the melody phrase by phrase.

Building a melody involves balancing phrases and then developing them into sections.

Working on different ways of developing your melody.

Develop the hook; experiment with sequences, or scale and arpeggio patterns; know when to write a simple melody; work on the climax of the song; include some contrast; add a surprise.

Avoiding problems.

Keep a sense of direction; make sure that the phrases balance; write within a comfortable vocal range; write a singable melodic line; make sure that the melody communicates the message of the song and be creative.

EXERCISES

1. **Writing melodic hooks**
    - Write a new melodic hook to the following phrases that have come out of Hillsong worship songs. Try to illustrate the words in a memorable and fresh way.
    - 'Shout to the Lord'; 'Calvary covers it all'; 'Christ is enough for me'
    - Write a melodic hook using the following interval leaps as part of it.

    An octave jump either up or down. e.g. C to C

    A rising minor 7th. e.g. C to Bb

    A descending perfect 4th. e.g. C to G.

2. **Building a melody**
    - Write a two bar melodic phrase as the beginning of a chorus. Think about the

- direction that it is going in. Think about the hook.
- Write another two bar phrase that balances it.
- Develop your four bar phrase with another four bars using the same technique.

3. Developing a melody

- Using one of your melodic hooks develop it in the following ways. Either repeat it but change one of the intervals or repeat it at a higher or lower pitch.
- Develop one of your hooks into a sequence with 3 repetitions but be careful not to change key as you do so. This will involve slight adjustments to the hook each time.

4. Completing the melody

- Analyse the 8 bar melody that you wrote in the exercises at the end of Section 2. Are the intervals large or small? What is the general pitch of the melody? What is the rhythmic pattern?
- Write a verse to go with your chorus that contrasts with it.
- What key have you written your melody in? What key would it be in if it needed to be transposed down a tone for a small group to sing?

CHAPTER 15

FILLING IN THE HARMONY

I like colour. I like the vibrant purple of the jacaranda flower and the bold red of a flame tree but I also like the more muted grey-green of the eucalyptus and the warm browns and oranges of an English autumn. My taste is reflected in the way I dress, the way I decorate my house and the artists I enjoy and it probably says something about the type of person I am. People tend to have strong views on the colours they like or dislike and how they should be used and a grey world with no variation in colour would be a duller place to live in. When I look at creation I think that God likes colour too.

So why am I talking about colour in a chapter on harmony? Well, in many ways, harmony is what gives the colour to music. You only have to listen to a jazz musician playing a well-known melody to hear how different it can sound with new chords underneath it. In this chapter we will catch a glimpse of the amazing richness and variety of colours that different chords can bring to the simplest of melodies and the way in which these colours can help to illustrate the message of the song.

'For me, harmony, at its best comes from inspiration.
Harmony is a feeling – a mood, and you need to capture it.'
Raymond Badham

THOUGHTS ON HARMONY

Before we look at the technical aspects of harmony it is helpful to consider harmony in its broader sense. If you are unsure of what I mean by some of the chords I'm referring to then come back to this section after you have read the technical section.

Harmony can help to create the mood of the song

The type of harmonies used can enhance the message and atmosphere of the song. Discords or chords that do not resolve to the tonic chord can create an atmosphere of tension. Chords that are voiced without the 3rd of the chord can create a very open, pure sound that leaves it somewhere between major and minor in feel. Chords with suspended 4ths and 6th s can create a warm, luxuriant sound

   e.g. 'Glorify Your Name' (Darlene Zschech, David Holmes) The verse is solidly in A major but then the chorus moves to the relative minor (F#m) before moving on to E major and back to A major for the verse. Possibly this floating around the key centres is what creates the ethereal sound that goes well with words that speak of having 'wings to fly'.

e.g. 'Mighty To Save' (Reuben Morgan, Ben Fielding) This song is in A major but the verse starts on chord IV (D) before resolving to I (A) which is unusual.

Harmony can help to reinforce the style of the music

Different musical styles tend to use different chords and chord progressions as part of what makes them distinctive. If you want to reproduce a particular style then it is important not to deviate too far from these chords. For example the Blues uses flattened 3^{rd}s and dominant 7^{th}s within a basic pattern of chords I, IV and V. A major 7th chord or an augmented chord would sound out of place in a typical 12 bar blues. In the same way the use of the Dorian mode immediately gives a song a traditional folk sound.

Harmony is morally neutral

We discussed earlier in the book the fact that music is neither good nor evil but that associations can influence our response to it. This is true not only of styles but also of the harmonies we use and people can have strong views on this subject. When I was a young Christian there was a belief in some church quarters that major keys were good and that minor keys were bad. I remember an older minister complaining whenever we sang a song in a minor key because he felt that it was depressing and negative. This theory originated from Greek philosophers who believed that some modes were good and some were evil. Later, the mediaeval church, which was heavily influenced by Greek philosophy, added its backing to this theory and labelled some modes and intervals as demonic. However there is no biblical support for this belief and as Christians we should be influenced neither by Greek philosophy nor superstitions.

Harmony in essence is simply the structure, functions and relationships of chords and has no deeper meaning than that.

What we do with the rich range of options available is up to us and what we are trying to communicate in our song.

Harmony is an essential part of rhythm

Where we change our chords and what those chords are is an important part of the rhythmic shape of a song. It is a chord change that often accentuates the strong beats in the bar or that stresses syncopation.

e.g. 'No Other Name' (Jonas Myrin, Joel Houston). In the verse, which has long sustained notes, the harmonies change almost on every syllable. However in the chorus which moves faster lyrically the chord changes are fewer and come on the accented beats and significant words 'eyes, world, Name' etc.

Harmony underlies and can become the inspiration for a melody

A strong chord progression can often suggest a melodic line. In fact many songwriters start writing songs by finding a chord progression and then move on from there. The well-known song 'Fly me to the moon' by Bart Howard is a great example of a song that is based on a chord progression that follows the circle of 5th s.

'I want to write songs that are interesting but not so interesting that someone who doesn't know anything about music can't sing the song...You're not writing for yourself or for musicians...you're writing for God and you're writing for people to worship God.' **Marty Sampson**

HARMONY AND WORSHIP SONGS

When it comes to using harmonies in our worship songs there are some points to keep in mind.

Make sure that your harmonies are contemporary

Be aware that specific chords and chord progressions can date when they become associated with a particular era. For example, Major 7th chords were very popular at one point but were then over-used and became a bit clichéd although now they seem to be coming back again. Listen to the sounds that are popular now. Obviously a chord can go out of favour and then be rediscovered by a later generation but we need to stay in touch with the sounds that are popular now. Generally, if you want to play safe without doing any research, the simpler triads that are based around the scale never go out of fashion but they can also be a little bland when there is so much colour to choose from.

Make sure that your harmonies are appropriate

Music is made up of light and dark just as a painting combines light and shadow. While harmony itself is neutral, minor keys tend to sound more melancholy and emotional than major keys and different chords create different effects. The focus must always be on whether the harmonies used are serving the message of the song. If your words are very upbeat and victorious then a minor key with a number of complex, dark chords may not be helpful. However this cannot be a hard and fast rule. Many Jewish songs are in minor keys and yet sound very joyful, especially when accompanied by a lively, driving rhythm.

Can we write songs for worship that reflect the move away from conventional major and minor tonality? The legacy of classical composers' experimentation with sounds is found today in film scores, computer games and even in alternative popular music and so it is not alien to our 21ˢᵗ century ears. Whether it is appropriate in worship choruses is another matter. My feeling is that generally congregations are more comfortable with a key centre even if it modulates occasionally and that a strong key centre makes the song easier to learn and remember.

Make sure that your harmonies are interesting

You would not usually paint a picture using only one colour, unless you are Picasso going through his blue period, and nor do you harmonise a song with only one chord unless you are looking for a particular effect. Interesting harmonies can add colour to a simple melody.

e.g. 'I Surrender' (Matt Crocker). The verse moves from I (Dm) to III maj7 (F maj7) 'Here I am down on my knees again' The F maj7 adds interest.

It is worth noting though that the more up tempo your song, the less harmonic colour you need. Because interest is generated through the rhythm in fast songs, complex harmonies can make the music sound too cluttered

e.g. 'Alive' (Aodhan King, Alexander Pappas) This up tempo song is also based around I, IV, V and vi (E, A, B and C#m) although interest is added by the fact that the verses and chorus start on vi before resolving to I.

Make sure that your harmonies are playable

A very complicated arrangement or very complex chords may mean your song has limited church use because not every church can draw on experienced and technically skilled musicians. If you write a song that relies too heavily on complex harmonies you will find that, if they are too difficult for the band, the musicians will tend to simplify the chords and your effect will be lost. If there is not much else of interest in the song then it may be so weakened as to be unusable.

'I had just started learning guitar, and I learned four chords…I started playing them and playing all the different songs that I knew would fit in the four chord progression, which is quite a lot of songs. And a line came with a melody and…then there were a lot of sections that pretty much just flowed together and made a worship song. Looking back I feel the first song was a gift from God. After the first song I feel like the hard work had just begun.' **Jonathon Douglass** on writing his first song.

SOME BASIC ELEMENTS OF HARMONY

What I want to do here is to point you towards different aspects of harmony without becoming too technical. There are a number of books on the market that will teach you about both the fundamentals and more specialised types of harmony and you can have fun experimenting. Below are some of the things you need to know in order to start putting chords to your songs.

The basic triads (3 note chords)

Triads are the building blocks of music and they consist of three pitches sounded simultaneously. The basic triad is formed from a root note with one note placed a major or minor third above the root and a second note placed a major or minor third above that. These basic triads can then be inverted or spaced however you want.

Note: A major third consists of 4 semitones (half steps). A minor third consists of 3 semitones (half steps). If you are not sure what a semitone (half step) is simply look at a keyboard. The distance between any two adjacent notes, black or white, is one semitone.

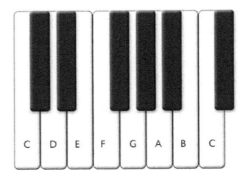

There are four types of basic triads (major, minor, diminished and augmented) and each one is constructed differently and each has a different sound and function. The two that are most significant if you are just starting out are the major and minor triads but I have included the others for the sake of completeness.

Major triads These are built as follows: Root + Major 3rd + Minor 3rd.

e.g. C,E,G　or D, F#, A or Bb, D, F.

The major triad has a bright sound and is the most popular of the basic triads.

Minor triads These are built as follows: Root + Minor 3rd + Major 3rd.

e.g. C,Eb,G or D, F,A or Bb, Db, F

In a major scale there are as many minor triads as major triads. The minor triad tends to have a more melancholy, emotional sound than the major triad.

Diminished triads These are built as follows: Root + Minor 3rd + Minor 3rd.

e.g. C, Eb, Gb or D, F, Ab or B, D, F

Augmented triads These are built as follows: Root + Major 3rd + Major 3rd.

e.g. C, E, G# or D, F#, A# or Bb, D, F#.

The Major Scale

Scales are the starting point for both melodies and chords so we need an understanding of scales in order to proceed.

The major scale is made up of the following steps: 1, 1, ½ , 1, 1, 1, ½ .

e.g. C major = C, D, E, F, G, A, B, C. (All the white notes on the piano)

The chords that are formed from the major scale

Songwriters generally select chords that are built on the notes of the key in which they are writing because the chords all relate well to one another. The seven chords that are built on the major scale include three major triads, three minor triads and one diminished triad. Out of these the most commonly used are chords built on the 1st, 2nd, 4th, 5th and 6th notes of the scale.

     e.g. C major: - C major, D minor, E minor, F major, G major, A minor, B diminished.

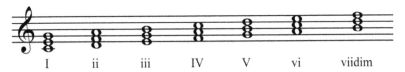

     I   ii   iii   IV   V   vi   viidim

You will notice that I have placed Roman numerals underneath the chords with the major chords in Upper Case and the minor chords in lower case. It is helpful to give chords numbers so that you can talk about the numerical relationship of chords across different keys. For example chords C, Dm and Em in the key of C major are equivalent to G, Am and Bm in the key of G major. If we label both sets I, ii and iii respectively in each case it is easier to see how the different chords work in different keys.

Simple chord combinations and progressions

If we return to our opening image of colours it is helpful to remember that some colours blend well while others clash. While we may sometimes choose to put red and orange together for effect when we put red with black or white it looks less shocking. In the same way some chords blend smoothly within a song while others can sound awkward even if they are part of the key that the song is written in.

A good chord progression is more important than any individual chord The way that chords fit together in a sequence is much more important than the sound of an individual chord. It is easy to become distracted by the sound of a complex chord and then to forget that it needs to go somewhere and to have a melody over it. The true power of harmony lies in how a chord relates to other chords.

The strongest progression is between chords I and V The smoothest blend comes between chords I and V and it is the strongest progression in Western music with chord V acting as a pull chord and chord I as a rest chord. Songs using only these two chords can work very successfully. Examples include the nursery rhyme 'Three blind mice' or the spiritual 'Joshua fought the battle of Jericho' (minor)

The combination of chords I, IV and V is a very popular one Many songs, especially folk music, Blues or Rock use only these three chords. Examples include 'Silent Night' (major) and 'Go down Moses' (minor).

Chords I, vi, ii or IV, and V work well together
e.g. 'Man Of Sorrows' (Matt Crocker, Brooke Ligertwood) This song uses just 4 chords I, IV, V and vi (F, Bb, C and Dm) Because this song is basically a modern hymn the lyrics are very important and the melody is quite classic in its structure so the simple chords complement that.

e.g. 'Cornerstone' (Jonas Myrin, Eric Liljero, Reuben Morgan) Again this modern hymn uses only four chords I, IV, V and vi (C, F, G and Am) although extra interest is added with a Csus4 chord at the end of the verse.

The relative minor chords make good substitutionary chords The transition between the two chords is very smooth and it is worth learning what they are especially if your song is sitting on one chord for a long time. You can then move to the relative minor and back again. In a major key (e.g. C major), chord vi (Am) is the relative minor of chord I (C); chord ii (Dm) is the relative minor of chord IV (F) and chord iii (Em) is the relative minor of chord V (G)

e.g. 'Ever Living God' (Raymond Badham) Raymond has used an E minor chord instead of the key chord which is G major and which creates a major/minor feel at the start of the song.

e.g. 'Transfiguration' (Brooke Ligertwood, Scott Ligertwood, Aodhan King, Taya Smith). The verse does not settle on the key chord I (C) but starts on ii7 (Dm7) and the chorus starts and ends on IV (F). It leaves us wondering what key the song is in. Is it C major or A natural minor? And maybe that reflects the mystery of the transfiguration.

e.g. 'Not Today' (Joel Houston, Matt Crocker). The verse uses only two chords   (F#m and A) and the effect is an ambiguity between whether it is in a major or minor key and maybe reflects the tension in the lyrics. However the chorus is more clearly in A major and that reflects the positive confession in the lyrics.

Turnarounds are important for songs or sections that are repeated A turnaround is the chord progression that will lead back into a repeat and it is important to find a series of chords that will lead back quickly and easily. e.g. ii, V or I, vi, IV,V.

'In Papua New Guinea, that's where I grew up, they play ukulele, guitar, and something they call "bamboo band' and so I learned how to play these instruments. My experience in Papua New Guinea gave me a great foundation in music theory. Back then, most people only knew three or four chords, so I got to know those few chords quite well, as well as their function in harmonic theory. My father ran a Bible College, so students would come from the various Provinces of PNG, bringing new musical styles and chords. We would spend hours at a time, playing and singing, often through into the night.' **Raymond Badham**

MORE ADVANCED ASPECTS OF HARMONY TO EXPLORE

Below are some suggestions about other areas of harmony that you may want to explore at some point. Again, I am only scratching the surface of what we could look at and I recommend studying more technical books to fill in the gaps.

Minor scales

Harmonic minor scale This scale is made up of the following steps: 1, ½, 1, 1, ½, 1 ½, ½. This is the main minor scale that is used in harmony today.

e.g. A harmonic minor = A. B, C, D, E, F, G#, A.

Melodic minor scale This scale differs according to whether it is ascending or descending. This is an interesting scale to use with its variation between the raised 6th and 7th tones ascending and the flattened 6th and 7th tones descending.

Ascending contains the following steps:1, ½ ,1, 1, 1, 1, ½ e.g. A, B, C, D, E, F#, G#, A.

Descending contains the following steps: 1, 1, ½ , 1, 1, ½ , 1. e.g. A, G. F, E, D, C,B, A.

Relative minor scale This is built using exactly the same notes as its relative major but it begins on the 6th tone of the major scale. The scale that is formed is called a natural minor scale and creates a modal, folk sound with its flattened 7th. Because there are no added accidentals (extra sharps or flats) it is easy to move from the major to the relative minor and back again.

e.g. The relative minor to C major is A minor and is made up of the following steps:

1, ½ ,1, 1, ½ , 1, 1. (A, B, C, D, E, F, G, A.)

Parallel minor scale This is also a natural minor but starts on the tonic of its parallel major. Switching from the major to its parallel minor and back again can create an interesting harmonic effect.

e.g. The parallel minor to C major is as follows: C, D, Eb, F, G, Ab, Bb, C

Triads built on notes of the minor scale

The seven triads are built on the notes of the harmonic minor scale. The chords include two minor chords, two major chords, 2 diminished and one augmented chords. The most commonly used chords in the minor scale are chords I, iv, V and VI.

e.g. A harmonic minor – Am, Bdim., C aug., Dm, E, F, G#dim.

There are some variations on the diminished and augmented chords used that, while not strictly speaking being part of the harmonic minor scale, can work well within the minor key because they relate to other forms of the minor scale.

The chord built on the second tone in the scale is altered to be played as a minor rather than a diminished chord so that it relates more to the melodic form of the minor scale.

e.g. In A minor B dim. becomes B minor.

The chord built on the third tone in the scale is altered to be played as a major rather than an augmented chord so that it relates more to the natural form of the minor scale.

e.g. In A minor Caug. becomes C major.

The seventh tone of the scale is also altered at times by being flattened by a half tone. In doing this the chord then becomes a major chord and relates to the natural form of the minor scale. Doing this creates a distinctive sound that is quite folky.

e.g. In A minor G#dim. becomes G major.

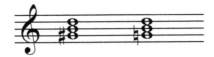

Four note and altered chords

I have focussed on simple three note triads because, if you know how to use them, you can harmonise any melody that you might write. However the permutations of what you could do harmonically is huge and I have included a few thoughts here.

Four note chords Basic 4 note chords include dominant 7[ths], diminished 7[ths], major 7[ths], major 6[ths] and minor 6[ths]. Some act as a pulling chord leading on to a resolution and others act as rest chords that do not need to move anywhere else. All of them add a richer texture to the music.

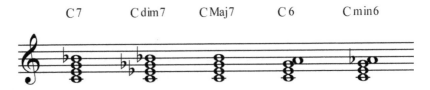

When using these chords remember that:

You can add a 6th, major 7th, or 9th to any major triad.

You can add a 6th, minor 7th, or 9th to most minor triads.

You can add a raised 5th, 6th, 9th, b9th to any dominant 7th.

You can add a 9th, b9th to any minor 7th.

Altered chords Chords may be altered with accidentals to make some exotic sounds especially in Jazz music.

e.g. Dom.7b5, Dom.7#5, Maj.7#5, Dom.7sus4 etc.

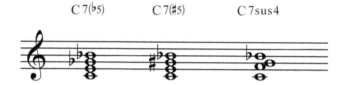

e.g. 'Passion' (Bede Benjamin-Korporall, Ben Tan, Laura Toggs, Aodhan King). This song uses a number of very interesting 4 note chords (F#m11; C#m7; Amaj9) as well as some altered chords (Dsus2; Bsus4) which all add to the harmonic colour of the song.

e.g. 'Heart Like Heaven' (Matt Crocker, Joel Houston). The bridge has some interesting 4 note chords including Gbmaj7, Ab6, and Ebm7.

Modes and less common scales

Modes Experiment with the different effects of modes especially with songs that you want to have an ethnic feel. The chords that are formed from the modes will be different from those formed by major and minor scales.

e.g. 'Forever And A Day' (Raymond Badham) Raymond's use of the G major   triad instead of G minor in the key of D minor implies the Dorian mode.

Less common scales The Pentatonic scale is the basis of Blues and can be found by simply playing the black notes on the keyboard.

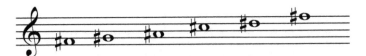

The chromatic scale is made up of all the half tones within an octave and can be useful in writing bass lines.

The Blues scale works with flattened 3rd, 5th and 7th that are bent rather than flattened the full half tone. The whole tone scale contains is made up entirely of whole tones, as the name suggests, and creates some interesting harmonies when chords are built on it.

Blues Scale

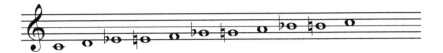

Whole Tone Scale

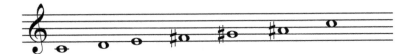

Modulation

Changing key can add greatly to the melodic interest of the song and it is worth learning how to do that successfully once you have mastered the basics of writing within a key.

'This is what I would call the psychology of tonality. This is creating a sense of home, going to an unknown territory, and then returning.'[23] Daniel Barenboim

Know how to work with the circle of fifths The circle of fifths is very useful in that you can enter and leave at any point so that your sequence of harmonies can vary in length. This circle shows us the relationship between keys.

e.g. The nearest keys to C major are F major (Bb) and G major (F#) and modulating to and from either of those is simply a matter of adding or removing the accidental. This is true wherever you start on the circle of keys.

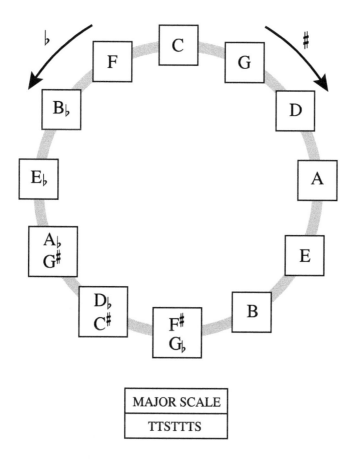

23 Daniel Barenboim and Edward W Said *Parallels and Paradoxes* Bloomsbury Publishing PLC UK 2002. p. 46

Near neighbours in modulation   Be aware of the natural relationships between keys. For example, C relates to its relative minor A minor. Adding a Bb to the key signature takes you to F major and adding an F# takes it to G major as its nearest relatives.

e.g. 'All I Need Is You' (Marty Sampson) Marty has written the verses in a minor key and then moved into the relative major on the chorus

Techniques of modulation It is helpful to know how to modulate by using a common note or the dominant of the new key. The chord progression ii, V, I is very useful. Alternatively you can simply shock the listener by changing key with little or no preparation but be prepared for the song to take a little longer to learn.

e.g. 'Song Of Freedom' (Marty Sampson) The change between the pre-chorus (C major) to the chorus (A major) is set up simply by a G triad which is the flattened 7th note in the new key and not what one would normally use.

e.g. 'To You Alone' (Reuben Morgan) Reuben uses a melodic and harmonic sequence on the verse that modulates from G major down a tone to F major and   back into G major for the chorus. The modulation back to G major is achieved by using the common note A that is the 3rd of the F triad and the 5th of the D triad. D is chord V in the key of G and so leads strongly back into that key.

Variants on standard major/minor tonality   Even though I think it is advisable to keep a conventional major/minor tonality we can make things more interesting by using devices such as pedal notes to create a certain tonal ambiguity or by leaving out the 3rd of the chord that would identify the song as major or minor. They offer an alternative to modulation as a way of adding harmonic interest to the song.

e.g. 'Highest' (Reuben Morgan) Reuben has used a pedal note underneath the first verse and chorus that anchors it to the key note regardless of the chords and melody above it. He moves away from that in the 2nd verse and chorus and creates a sense of development even though the melody stays the same.

e.g. 'Open Heaven (River Wild)' (Matt Crocker, Marty Sampson). The tonality of this song is made more interesting by the fact that the harmonies often seem at odds with the melody. For example in the verse we sing 'Spirit' (E to D) over the F chord which does not have either E or D in its triad. Then leading into the chorus 'Holy Spirit' (ACAG) is over Csus2 (made up of CDG) and we only really resolve that tension when we sing 'rain' (A) over the chord F. And this pattern continues creating a musical tension that echoes the mystery of the Holy Spirit who also does not fit into our nice little boxes.

Simple chord charts

I recommend that you look online to find a good programme such as noteflight.com or musescore.org that will help you.

On 'Open Heaven (River Wild)'

(MATT CROCKER, MARTY SAMPSON)

'Matt Crocker and I were writing and we had various song ideas we were working on. I left the room for five minutes and when I came back Matt said, 'What do you think about this?' He played the verse of 'Open Heaven' in its raw form. I was open to work on it and the song unraveled...This song tries to honour the Holy Spirit and His role in our lives and the Church (that is so often overlooked in my own personal life). It is a call to connect with what we believe God is seeking to achieve on Earth right now. It's an amazing thought that throughout the Bible, each generation were living in their

'present day' and often didn't realise what God was doing around them...This song is a call to our collective hearts to engage with God through the gift of His Holy Spirit.'
Marty Sampson

SUMMARY

Thoughts on harmony.

Harmony is morally neutral but helps to create the mood of a song and to reinforce a particular musical style. It is an essential part of rhythm and can inspire a melody.

Using harmony in worship songs.

Make sure that the chords used are contemporary, appropriate, interesting and playable.

Some basic elements of harmony

The basic triads, major scales and the chords formed from them and simple chord progressions.

More advanced aspects of harmony to explore.

Minor scales and the chords that are formed from them; four note and altered chords; modes and less common scales; modulation and chord charts.

EXERCISES

1. Working with chords I and V

Write a simple melody that only needs chords I and V to harmonise it.

2. Working with chords I, ii, IV,V and vi

Take the melody that you wrote in exercise 1 and substitute some of the original chords with chords ii, IV or vi.

3. Write a chord chart

Take the revised chords from Exercise 2 and put them into a simple chord chart.

CHAPTER 16

WORKING WITH RHYTHM

I n the chapter on the rhythm of words we considered the fact that rhythm is basically any pattern of weak and strong beats whether it is a ticking clock or the rhythm of speech. In this chapter we will take this concept further and consider musical rhythm and how we can use it effectively in our song writing.

Put at its simplest, musical rhythm is simply the way that sounds fills up a bar. The three major ingredients of music, namely melody, harmony and rhythm are all interdependent as it is the rhythmic pattern of the music as much as the melody that determines where the harmonies change and the placing of the strong accents inevitably affects the shape of the melody.

'The most important thing to remember about rhythm is the balance between repetition and interest.' **Reuben Morgan**

RHYTHM AND WORSHIP SONGS

Rhythm may not be the most important element of your song but it has the potential to enhance or derail it if not used carefully.

Make sure that your rhythms are contemporary

Rhythm dates very fast and although this does not matter with choruses that tend to have a short life it does matter if we are writing hymns or songs that are intended to last. Particular rhythmic patterns tend to become strongly associated with a period in music (e.g. swing) and therefore songs based on them will date as soon as the style goes out of fashion. When drawing from contemporary rhythms be careful not to plagiarise by copying a particular song too closely.

Make sure that your rhythms are appropriate

Make the rhythm appropriate to the message of the song. A song with a disco beat that speaks of the Cross is going to cut across the message because its dance associations do not reflect the seriousness of the topic.

Make sure that your rhythms are interesting

This is especially important if the hook of your song is based around a rhythmic pattern rather than a melody. We will look at some of the ways that we can do that later in the chapter but it is helpful to think about elements such as syncopation, different time signatures, layers of rhythm and instrumentation when working to make your rhythms interesting.

e.g. 'Let There Be Light' (, Matthew Crocker, Joel Houston, Michael Guy Chislett Brooke Ligertwood, Scott Ligertwood, Jonas Myrin). The statement 'Let there be light' in the chorus anticipates the downbeat and makes it very memorable and dramatic.

e.g. 'Wake' (Joel Davies, Hannah Hobbs, Alex Pappas). Singing 'wake within me' on the off beat in the chorus is unexpected.

'Wake' is a song I co-wrote with Joel Davies and Alex Pappas. This was an exciting process as we were experimenting with a style of music that, at the time, was completely new to us. It was fun and we truly didn't know whether people would take to the song or not. It felt exciting and risky to try writing in a genre and style we hadn't used before.' **Hannah Hobbs**

Make sure that your rhythms are playable and singable

Be aware of the limitations of most church bands. Don't aim for too much rhythmic complexity as an essential part of the song. Will the song work with just a guitar, bass and drums if all the layers are stripped away?

Church goers can cope with singing syncopated beats more easily than previous generations could because so much popular music uses it and they are used to hearing it. However we need to be careful not to assume too high a performance level especially as congregations are not comprised solely of young people. It is one thing to listen to complicated rhythms and quite another to sing them.

ASPECTS OF RHYTHM TO EXPLORE AND DEVELOP

This is not an exhaustive look at rhythm but it will hopefully get you thinking more widely about what is possible.

Master the terms

Rhythm is the distribution of sound over time.

A Beat is a unit of measurement When writing a song it is best to find the beat first and then find a time signature to fit. The speed of the beat will affect the feel of the song.

The Tempo is the speed of the beat. Tempo used to be indicated by various Italian words such as 'lento' = slow or 'allegro' = fast. The problem with these terms was that the interpretation of how slow 'lento' was, for example, depended on the performer. Today we tend to be more specific in our instructions by indicating how many beats there are in a minute. This in turn can be measured by a metronome. The term 'up tempo' indicates a beat speed that is 120 quarter notes a minute or faster.

The Metre is the way the accents fall This is very important since it affects the stresses of the words. Important words should fall on the first beat of the bar. The most common metres are 3 and 4 with the main accent on the first beat of the bar.

'I think tempo can really affect if people will be able to engage with the song in a corporate setting. We work really hard to make sure it "feels right"' **Jonathon Douglass**

Understand the fundamentals

If you have never studied the basics of rhythm and rhythmic notation it would be a good idea to invest in a book that covers the rudiments of music theory. It is actually very simple and mathematically logical once you have mastered the language.

I find it easier to work with the concept of whole, half, quarter and eighth notes rather than the more traditional semibreve, minim, crotchet and quaver.

One thing that I do want to say is that an ability to hear and feel rhythm is far more important that knowing how to write it. There is no substitute for listening to as much music as you can and trying to work out what is going on rhythmically. I have made some suggestions on how you might do that at the end of Chapter 19.

Experiment with different time signatures

Different time signatures can create different effects and moods. You will also notice that I have used a number of examples of songs that are not worship songs in this section. This is because worship songs typically favour the standard 4/4 time signature with occasional moves into compound time. However there is no reason why other time signatures could not work either for the whole song or for parts of a song.

Simple time signatures In simple time signatures the beat is divided and subdivided by two.

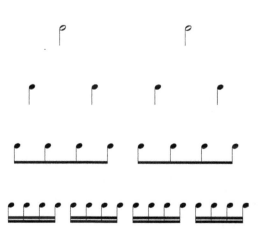

4/4 The most common time signature for worship songs is 4/4 and its regular pattern that divides the bar in half works well in songs. Mathematically the four beats complement the four bar phrases that most songs are also built on and that may be why songwriters naturally seem to gravitate towards it. Certainly if you are writing your first few songs this is a great time signature to work with. Remember that the first beat of the bar is the strongest and then the 3rd beat has the next strongest accent unless you are using syncopation.

2/4 This works in a similar fashion to 4/4 but with only one accented beat in the bar.

3/4 Three beats in a bar creates a lilting beat that is very attractive. It has been associated traditionally with the waltz but can work very well in songs and allows for a different melodic and harmonic structure. It is probably better suited to slower songs. The Jazz waltz alternative is also worth exploring.

e.g. 'Close Every Door To Me' (Lloyd Webber/Rice from 'Joseph And His Amazing Technicolour Dreamcoat')

e.g 'My Favourite Things' (Rodgers/Hammerstein from 'The Sound Of Music')

5/4, 7/4 Notice how these two time signatures throw the listener off balance. In 5/4 time it is because there seems to be an extra beat and in 7/4 time it is because there seems to be a beat missing. These time signatures are unlikely to be used for an entire worship song because of the difficulty that bands and singers would have in playing and singing them. However you may choose to write occasional bars or even sections in one of these time signatures for a particular effect.

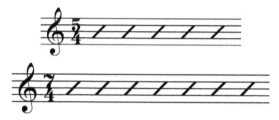

e.g. 'Everything's Alright' (Lloyd Webber/Rice from 'Jesus Christ Superstar') is in 5/4 time. Usually there is a secondary accent on either the 3rd or 4th beat as well as the strong 1st beat.

'Temple Song' (Lloyd Webber/Rice from 'Jesus Christ Superstar') is in 7/4 time. Here the secondary accent tends to fall on either the 4th or 5th beat.

Compound time signatures In compound time the beat is divided into three and then those divisions are divided and subdivided by two as in simple time.

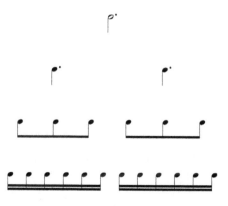

6/8   This corresponds to 2/4 in simple time. In 6/8 time the accents usually fall on the 1ˢᵗ and 4ᵗʰ of the six but an interesting and syncopated feel can be created by mixing the 1ˢᵗ and 3ʳᵈ feel with 1ˢᵗ,3ʳᵈ and 5ᵗʰ.

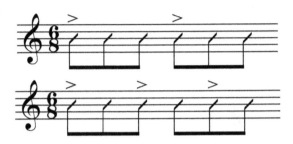

e.g. 'Captain' (Benjamin Hastings, Seth Simmons)

e.g. 'His Glory Appears' (Marty Sampson, Darlene Zschech)

9/8 and 12/8   These correspond to the triple and quadruple simple times.

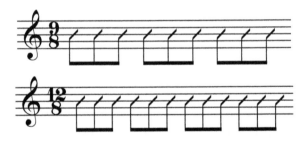

e.g. 'Your Word' (Chris Davenport) 12/8

Chart comparing simple and compound times.

Simple Time				Compound Time		
2/2	2/4	2/8	corresponds to	6/4	6/8	6/16
3/2	3/4	3/8	corresponds to	9/4	9/8	9/16
4/2	4/4	4/8	corresponds to	12/4	12/8	12/16

Note: It will be helpful also to know about dotted and tied notes and about using triplet patterns in simple and compound time signatures.

e.g. 'Not Today' (Joel Houston, Matt Crocker) The song is in standard 4/4 time but the use of a dotted quaver + dotted quaver + quaver almost gives it a sense of compound time and drives the melody forward.

Experiment with changing the time signature during a song

This can add interest and contrast during the course of a song. It also prevents the rhythm from becoming too rigid and repetitive and allow room for the lyric rhythm to shape the music.

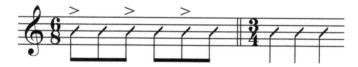

e.g. 'America' (Leonard Bernstein and Stephen Sondheim from 'West Side Story') This song uses alternating 6/8 and 3/4 bars to great effect.

e.g. 'Soldier' (Tulele Faletolu, Marty Sampson) In the chorus the time signature varies between 4/4 and 3/4 on the words 'All the world can't stop, can't stop Him'

Syncopation

In syncopation an accent is put on a part of thwe bar which is not regularly important. What this means is that the accent is moved from the strong to what is usually the weak beat. This upsets our sense of balance and adds interest. Syncopation is important in jazz, soul, blues and pop but less so in heavy metal and acid rock which depends more on a driving rhythm on the beat. In syncopation we need to hear the contrast with the ON beat. One common technique in Western music is to anticipate the first beat of the bar.

e.g. 'In Control' (Ben Fielding, Aodhan King) The beat is anticipated in the chorus.

e.g. 'Grace To Grace' (Chris Davenport, Joel Houston) There are some interesting syncopations throughout this song.

e.g. 'As It Is (In Heaven)' (Joel Houston, Ben Fielding) In the chorus the word 'fail' falls just before the downbeat whereas in the previous lines 'love, found, saved' all fall on the beat.

e.g. 'No Other Name' (Jonas Myrin, Joel Houston). The penultimate line on the first two verses delays the final word (heart, kings) but on the 3rd verse 'Name' is sung on the beat stressing the major thought of the song.

e.g. 'Open Heaven (River Wild)' (Matt Crocker, Marty Sampson) In the chorus 'Oh Holy Spirit, Burn like a fire/All consuming/Consume me.' Whereas 'Oh' and 'Burn' are stressed syllables 'all consuming' follows a rest and comes on the off beat.

e.g. 'Alive' (Aodhan King, Alexander Pappas) There are some interesting syncopations in the pre chorus and chorus that add to the energy of the song.

Use layers of rhythms to add interest to your music

Study how to build up layers of rhythms and counter rhythms. This will make a simple song exciting. Even with the limitations of many church bands there is a lot that can be done with a bass, drums and guitar in layers of rhythm.

e.g. 'Your Word' (Chris Davenport) Chris uses contra rhythms in the instruments below the vocal.

Experiment with the rhythm patterns of other cultures

There is such a rich variety of rhythmic patterns and different instruments in world music that can add interest to your song writing even if you do not take on the whole style. When thinking about rhythm listen especially to African and Latin American music. Many multi-cultural churches deliberately use the rhythm patterns of other cultures within their congregation to great effect.

Cha Cha

Mambo

Tango

'To write up-tempo songs, you need to know, at least a little, how the drums work.' **Raymond Badham**

Use the Tools

Use a metronome Remember that the metronome is a useful tool but it is important to develop a feeling for tempo yourself that is not reliant on the beeping of a machine.

Learn to use a drum machine or drum loops on software

programmes These are particularly helpful when you are experimenting with rhythm patterns that are unfamiliar to you since you can set the beat and then work on your melody and harmonies.

Learn the basics about the rhythm section of a band, especially the drums When you understand how the different percussion instruments work together with the bass and keyboard to form a rhythmic platform that will help you to add the interest of layers of rhythm in your songs.

Remember that silence as well as sound is a part of rhythm

Just as we have talked about leaving space in our lyrics for the music so we also need to leave space in our music at times or it will sound cluttered. One of the great faults of an inexperienced band is that everyone plays all the time! As songwriters we can include silence in various ways.

Use long, sustained notes You may choose to use some long, sustained notes without much underneath them that will give a sense of rest and space. The sound continues but it is not being driven forward rhythmically.

e.g. 'Passion' (Bede Benjamin-Korporall, Ben Tan, Laura Toggs, Aodhan King) In the 2nd bridge the lyrics 'I love you' are sung on sustained notes.

Have a complete break in the song You may choose to have a complete break in the music (technically known as a rest) which allows for a moment of silence. The advantage of a rest is that when the music starts again it comes in with a new energy and this can be useful if you are starting a contrasting section. The danger is that too long a break will rob the song of energy. Silence has to be used sparingly and carefully for it to be effective.

e.g. 'Empires' (Joel Houston, Dylan Thomas, Chris Davenport,

Ben Tennikoff). The vocal line has a number of rests in it especially after the end of the 2nd line 'Empires of dirt and grace'. The music continues underneath so it is not complete silence but it does allow the congregation to reflect on what they have just sung in a song that has some very thought provoking lyrics.

'Rhythm is essential to the flow and feel of a song. A whole song can become pleasant or unpleasant as a result of the rhythm. Experiment with rhythm and you find your musical mind stretches as a result. This is one of the unseen factors in song writing. Amazing songs FEEL good, and that's the result of GREAT rhythm.' **Marty Sampson**

SUMMARY

When writing worship songs make sure that the rhythms you use are contemporary, appropriate, interesting and playable.

Aspects of rhythm to explore and develop include:

Mastering the terms.

These terms include the beat, tempo and metre.

Understanding the fundamentals

Learn the language of musical rhythm

Experimenting with different time signatures

This includes both simple and compound time.

Changing time signatures.

This may involve time signature changes between sections or bar to bar.

Working with syncopation

Syncopation adds interest by upsetting our sense of balance.

Using layers of rhythm

Use the instruments at your disposal creatively.

Trying out rhythm patterns of other cultures

Allow your thinking to be stretched by listening widely.

Making effective use of rhythmic instruments and tools.

The more you understand the more you can do.

Remembering that silence is also a part of rhythm

Using rests prevents the music from becoming too busy or cluttered.

EXERCISES

1. **Clapping rhythms** (This exercise needs two people)

   The best way to get a feel for different rhythm patterns is to play or clap them. Find a song that you know and have one person clapping the basic beat while the other person claps the rhythms of the melody against it. Take turns in clapping the more difficult part. Gradually progress to more complicated songs that include syncopation and simple and compound times.

2. **Write a rhythmic hook for lyrics** (This exercise needs two people)

   Again work with a partner and, while one person claps four beats in a bar the other one tries out different patterns. Take turns so that you each find a rhythmic hook.

   Set some words to it that could be a lyric hook.

3. **Write a rhythmic hook for the band.**

   A strong rhythmic instrumental hook can often help to make a song memorable.

   Go back to one of the songs that you have been working on in earlier chapters and develop a rhythmic pattern that could complement the rhythm of your melody.

IMPROVING
YOUR SONG

On 'Mighty To Save' (Reuben Morgan, Ben Fielding)

'This song flowed from a conversation about what was going to be
helpful for church to sing in that season. Ben Fielding and I talked
about it being singable for the congregation and for the themes to be
at its foundation what every Christian believes. That it landed as a
salvation song, fit the brief ultimately. Neither of us were convinced we
nailed the brief but we attempted it.

The song was written over a process of about three months. The most
challenging part of the process was finding the right starting point that
we both agreed on which happened to be the chorus. From then each
section had its own journey of weighing up many different versions

against the others…This song is a lesson in knowing what you're going for and not settling. I strongly believe the Holy Spirit guides the process, through the details and the moments even when we are not aware of Him.'

Reuben Morgan

'The art of song writing for me is in the revision. I'll often get bursts of creativity, whether it's a thought, a lyric or a melody, or all of that together in a few minutes and I feel like I have a song. But it's then that the labour begins…formulating and putting the last bits of the puzzle in place; the right lyric correspondence to the right melody, moulding it, chipping away the rough bits, getting it right can take weeks, months and sometimes years. That's the art, and that's the discipline. It can be frustrating, but it's worth it when the last piece of the puzzle fits and you see the finished picture.'

Joel Houston

CHAPTER 17

REVISE, REWORK, REWRITE!

'A good song is not written. It is re-written.' That was the catch phrase that I belaboured my poor students with throughout the years that I taught song writing. I'm not sure who originally said it but it expresses a valuable truth and balances the mythology that a song that is written quickly is somehow more inspired than a song that has been laboured over and reworked.

Of course there are always exceptions. We've all heard of songs that were written in twenty minutes and sung around the world. Handel's 'Messiah' was written in a week! But the exceptions simply prove the rule. Handel may have written under incredible inspiration but he was writing out of years of experience as a composer. The worship song that comes fully-fledged out of a time of private devotion usually comes on the back of years of song writing and time spent with God. We do not work in a vacuum. And even those songs that are written quickly and under inspiration are often fine-tuned and reworked as they are arranged and recorded. The revising sometimes goes on almost unnoticed but it is there just the same.

On the other hand I have heard a large number of songs that were written quickly and without revision and they sound like it! They are excused with pseudo spiritual arguments such as 'How can I change what God gave me?' 'This is what I sang in the spirit so it can't be changed.' These writers tend to think that true genius is spontaneous and that there will be no need to plan or to revise. However although the idea may be 'inspired' the responsibility to organise that idea is the writer's. When you study the prophetic books they reflect careful structuring and thought. God inspires but He works through human abilities and gifts.

The message does not change but the vehicle that delivers the message can be fine-tuned and revised until it is as good as you can make it. My husband, Robert is an excellent preacher and over the years I have watched as he has worked on his sermons. Once he knows what God has put on his spirit he then spends hours and even weeks working on the structure and content of the message. He believes that there is always a perfect, beautiful, satisfying way to structure and express a sermon. He is not satisfied with an approximation or with something that does not fit but continues to work until he finds what he knows must be there.

It is the same with song writing. It is so easy to settle for something that will do but which may not be the best and then to excuse your laziness by spiritualising it! Joel Houston is a great example of a songwriter who is never prepared to settle for near enough is good enough. He can write literally dozens of versions of lyrics to one song before he is satisfied.

Our challenge as songwriters is to write our best songs for worship and not to settle for mediocrity. With a few exceptions, most songs do not come easily and so to settle for a first draft is usually to settle for something that is less than it could be if more time were taken to work on it. As we listen to the Holy Spirit and, at the same time, develop our skills God is able to use us to greater and greater effect.

'When I begin the writing process, I sit down and just write down ideas…Most of the ideas come pretty quick and I get most of them in a couple of minutes. I find that the best thing to do is just to roll with it because it generally doesn't last very long! I try to get down as much as I can when I am in this phase and usually I put down a verse and chorus. Once I have that down, it is pretty well the song and then I begin the rewriting. I find that rewriting is always a much longer process and it could take weeks.' **Reuben Morgan**

REVISION CHECK LIST

Most of these points have been covered in more detail in other chapters so I have simply outlined them here.

Don't throw anything away

Cross out in pencil. If you are working on computer, print all your versions. Often an idea, discarded earlier, fits a later version of the song or even another song altogether.

Finish your first draft before revising

When you are first working on your song don't be too critical or you may miss the overall flow of the song by becoming too involved in the details. It is when that initial stage is over that you start revising and tidying up.

Check the marriage of the words and music

Do the words and music complement one another emotionally or do they clash?

On 'Real Love'
(MICHAEL FATKIN, HANNAH HOBBS, ALEX PAPPAS)

'Love can mean so many different things to people so we were inspired to write around the love of Jesus being the most real love of all. The song is upbeat so we wanted the lyrics to have a sense of joy about them. The process was quite long and included plenty of re-writing ideas until we finally landed on something we felt was ready.' **Hannah Hobbs**

Ask others for their opinions and accept criticism gratefully and graciously

Don't be easily satisfied. Play your song to people who will be honest with you and give you a fair criticism. The trouble is that we often play our songs to our best friends who are either so impressed that we have written anything at all or are too close to us to give us an honest opinion. Play it to people who know what they are talking about. Remember that judging songs is subjective and not everyone will love your song. However there are certain qualities that make a song a good one and these can be assessed objectively.

Learn to critique songs yourself

Play songs that have influenced your own life and try to work out why that is and what makes them good songs. Ask yourself what could be done to improve them. When I hear a new worship chorus, at some point I always find myself analysing it and thinking about what I would suggest if it had been submitted to me in one of my classes. Learn to be a constructive critic of both your own and others' songs.

Being a constructive critic is more than saying that you like or don't like a song. It involves making specific positive comments on the song and specific suggestions for improvement. Think about how you would like someone to respond to a song that you have poured your heart into.

'You never 100% know if a song is completely finished or not, and this is why it is so important to revise, rework, and rewrite whatever song you are working on. The more time you invest into an idea, the more kinks you will find to iron out. I have the privilege of writing with Joel Houston from time to time, and he is one of the most diligent people I know when it comes to revising and rewriting a song that he is working on. As a writer, we should see ourselves as artists. And why on earth would you want to put a work of art out for others to see or hear, unless it's the absolute best it can be.' **Matt Crocker**

Work on every element in your song

Look at each element of your song and work on improving it. e.g. Harmony: Are there other chords that you could use that would enhance the message of the song or give it more colour? e.g. Lyrics: Are there wrong stresses or clichés?

The final 2% of a song almost invariably takes the longest time to write. These are the final lyric changes, the alteration of melody or harmony that has the potential to take a song from being a good song to a great song. This is where all the tools of songwriting that we have learnt along the way are put to work.' **Ben Fielding**

Allow your song the test of time

When you write a song go away and leave it for a while and then come back to it with a fresh ear and see where changes might be made. It is much harder to be objective about something you have just been working on.

Seek to be fresh and original in your expression

If your song sounds very familiar the chances are that it is! Work to break out of your normal mould.

Check that you are communicating clearly

Is your original concept still strong or have you lost sight of it as the song progressed?

Listen to the Holy Spirit

Are you taking time to pray about this song? What is the Holy Spirit, Who is the source of all inspiration, saying to you?

CHAPTER 18

CO-WRITING
A SONG

The musical world is full of great songwriting teams. Successful partnerships include Rodgers and Hammerstein, Boulbil and Schonberg, Sondheim and Bernstein, Lloyd Webber and Rice, Elton John and Bernie Taupin, and Lennon and McCartney among many others. The practice of pairing a lyricist with a composer is not a new one but goes back for centuries. Many, possibly most, of our songs that come out of Hillsong church are co-written these days often by a number of people as you've probably noticed while you've been reading the book. The fact that it is so widespread would seem to argue for its value as a practice and we will consider some of the reasons in this chapter.

Most of my experience of co-writing came over the years when I wrote an annual musical for the college students to perform. I would write the script and then the students and I would write the songs, either individually, or in pairs. We would meet as a group and listen to each other's songs and make suggestions and alterations. I never really felt like the teacher in these times but simply a fellow writer, although I have to admit that I had the final say! It was an enriching and exhilarating experience and one that I would highly recommend.

WHY CO-WRITE?

'Two are better than one, because they have a good return for their work' (Ecclesiastes 4:9 NIV)

Co-writing can be great for people who have complementary songwriting strengths

While I trained as a musician, my great passion is words and I can struggle at times over the music. I find it easier to put words to music rather than the other way around. I have other friends who have melodies coming out of every pore but who agonise over writing the lyrics. That is not to say that I can never write melodies, because I have, or that my friends cannot come up with some great lyrics, because they do, but sometimes it can be good to pool our strengths.

Co-writing can help to deal with writer's block

If you have a great idea that has sat on your phone or in your notepad because you are stuck then another person's perspective can be all it takes. My husband is great at that. Although not a trained musician he has an ear for what works and a creative mind that can often spark ideas. Co-writing can be as unstructured as a few of you sitting over a coffee and tossing ideas around.

Co-writing can make a good song into an excellent one

'As iron sharpens iron, so one man sharpens another.' (Proverbs 27:17 NIV)

There is such a fine line between a good song and a song that has a touch of greatness about it. A co-writer who refuses to allow you to settle for an ordinary lyric or an average melody can make that difference.

Co-writing can be fun

If you find the right person it can be a very enjoyable experience to collaborate on something creative. Those brainstorming times when anything and everything is thrown into the mix and passions run high can be so exciting.

I remember writing a song with one of my students who was going to be singing this particular song in the musical. We were discussing the lyrics that I had written and he challenged a phrase I had written as not being something that his character would say. For me that was a wonderful moment because, although I had written the script and created this character, suddenly a new dimension was added.

WHO SHOULD YOU WRITE WITH?

It may take a few attempts to find someone that you feel comfortable with as a co-writer. Do not give up too quickly but keep looking. Here are a few important factors to consider.

Look for someone who is compatible spiritually

This is not like writing a commercial pop song when you simply advertise in a music store or industry magazine for a lyricist or musician. You are writing worship songs and so you need someone who is on the same spiritual wavelength as you are. I am not talking about the same spiritual maturity or denominational background but about a shared passion for Jesus and for worshipping in spirit and in truth. You may end up writing with someone who has only just started out on their journey as a songwriter or as a Christian but their heart is in tune with yours and they have a freshness to contribute that you may have lost.

Look for someone who is compatible relationally

You need to be able to communicate directly and honestly with your fellow writer or your collaboration is not going to work. Failures of communication can result in wasted hours working at cross purposes or in unnecessary offence. Some people write wonderfully creative songs but cannot express what is in their heads. If you find yourself working with someone like that you will either need endless patience and wisdom to convert their ideas into words or you may need to leave them to keep creating on their own and find someone who speaks the same language as you.

This area is also linked to that of respect. I think it is essential that you respect not only the gift that your co-writer has but also the person. If you do not like or respect your co-writer that is bound to affect your work together.

Look for someone who is compatible creatively

People have different ways of working as we will see when we look at the guidelines. If you are the sort of person who needs to work on every note of the song in close proximity with your co-writer do not choose someone whose idea of co-writing is brief discussions but essentially working on his or her own. Talk about your work habits before you ever start and then you will avoid wasting time and energy on a partnership that is never going to work.

'*The concept of co-writing has made all of our songs better.
I am the songwriter I am because of the input of my peers and
leaders.*' **Jonathon Douglass**

GUIDELINES FOR CO-WRITING

Personally I work best when I have a brief discussion with my co-writer followed by time on my own to work on the song, preferably the lyrics. Then we meet again and see how the song has progressed. I find that I do not think well when other people are around and so the hard work of the creativity needs to happen in isolation. For other people it can be exactly the opposite which leads to my first guideline.

There are no rules

How you go about writing with someone else is entirely up to the two of you. There are no rules about whether the words or melody should come first or whether one person should write all the lyrics and the other all the music. There are no rules about whether you should work in the same room or apart. There are no rules either about the extent of the collaboration. Co-writing can be as minimal as listening to a song someone else has already written and making constructive suggestions about changes or as extensive as sitting together and working on every word and note. It can be spontaneous in that you may happen to be discussing an idea for a song and then just pick up a guitar and start writing or it may be a formal arrangement with set times for working and discussion and a plan to write a particular type of song.

On 'Thank You Jesus' (Matt Crocker, Hannah Hobbs)

'Toward the beginning of 2013, a group of songwriters from our church put some days aside to spend time collaborating and seeking God for new songs…On the second day, Matty Crocker and I started our session; it was the first time we had ever written together. As a songwriter, you always hope that every writing session leads to an incredible song, but unfortunately it doesn't always happen. That day, however, I think Matt and I both knew we had come across something special…The idea was sparked from a comment that our Creative Pastor Cass Langton, made about how it would be great to have a 'Thank You' song in church. A song themed around the message of gratitude towards God. From there we began to work on a chorus that simply said: 'Thank You Jesus, You set me free. Christ my Saviour You rescued me'[12]

Hannah Hobbs

Use constructive not destructive criticism

Presenting a song or creative idea is a very vulnerable thing to do. What we create is so much a part of our identity that an attack on our song can feel like an attack on us. I used to deliberately play some of my songs to my songwriting students in order to identify with the vulnerability they felt when they submitted their songs to me for marking. The key is to offer constructive criticism. When

I asked my students to comment on other students' work I asked them firstly to say what they liked about the song and secondly what they would improve rather than what they did not like.

When we are on the receiving end of comments we need to learn not to become defensive but to listen carefully to what is being said. One thing we must not do is counter attack if we feel that we are being unfairly criticized. Responding with 'Well, I think your melody is rubbish' is not going to help your working relationship! In the end it comes down to courtesy and sensitivity when speaking about your co-writer's work and humility and willingness to change when it comes to hearing about your own.

'Be a contributor not just a critic. Have fun and work hard at keeping the atmosphere of your writing session positive. It is so easy to comment on the thing we don't like but often more difficult to come up with ideas that we love. Don't be afraid to put an idea out there in a co-writing session. Even if it is not the greatest idea, it sometimes helps to step out and get the momentum of a session rolling. You never know, it could lead to something special. Respect that every writer, no matter what their level of experience, has something unique to bring to the table.' **Hannah Hobbs**

Allow enough time

As with any songwriting it is easy to be overly impressed with your first effort especially if you are both pleased with it. Take the time to go away and reflect on the song and come back in the cold light of another day and look at it with fresh eyes. Generally, once the first thrill of creativity is over is when the weaknesses in the song become apparent and you can begin to craft it more precisely.

It is important also to respect each other's time. We all lead full lives and so punctuality is only polite when you are working with someone else. Equally, if the agreement was that one of you would come with a set of lyrics or a melody then do not turn up hoping that something will materialize out of thin air once you are together. If we value one another we will not waste their time.

Agree to agree

If this is going to be a song that carries both your names then you both need to be happy with every aspect of the song. You need to agree that if one person is not happy with an element that you have been working on that you will change it. If you have a fairly strong or dominant personality and your co-writer is either very easy going or non- assertive you need to be careful to make sure that you really have reached an agreement.

Have a generous heart

Over the years I have, both as a teacher and a friend, had input into hundreds of songs and many of them have gone on to be recorded. But I do not consider making the odd lyric or musical suggestion to be co-writing or insist on recognition for it. When we become too legalistic or greedy about wanting our percentage of the royalties of a song that has been written we have moved far away from the spirit that should be behind writing songs for worship. After all, who inspires the songs in the first place? This is not to say that we cannot be professional about our writing (see Chapter 20 on the Business of Songwriting). It is important to have integrity and to recognise the contribution of others but, when it comes to our own contribution, we need a generosity of spirit.

Keep your purpose in mind

Make sure that you keep revisiting the original concept and message of the song so that you do not lose your focus once you become caught up in the creativity of the moment. It is a good idea, at the start, to write down a brief sentence that encapsulates the message of the song. This will then serve not only as a reference point while you are writing but also to make sure that you have both understood what the song is about.

On 'Cornerstone'
(JONAS MYRIN, ERIC LILJERO, REUBEN MORGAN)

'As a songwriter I've been blessed to co-write with some of my favourite Christian songwriters ever. Jonas Myrin would be one of them. We wrote 'Cornerstone' in an old church building in the centre of Stockholm with our good friend Eric, who is also an outstanding writer and leader. Jonas came with the idea of writing a song out of this hymn that he'd found, and he had made a good start on the process. The song emerged as a response to a tragedy that occurred at that time in Norway, and so we were talking and thinking about what is the best thing people could sing in this situation. The song came together in one session. We worked and moulded the melody so that it could fit the original verses. I still remember the moment when Jonas spontaneously started singing over and over the line: 'Christ alone, Cornerstone, Christ alone, Cornerstone,' and we ran with it from there, shaping the rest of the lyric and the melody for the chorus.' **Reuben Morgan**

SUMMARY

Co-writing has been a widespread practice throughout the history of songwriting.

Why co-write?

It can be work well when there are complementary songwriting strengths; it can help to deal with writer's block; it can make a good song into a great one and it can be fun.

Who should you write with?

Look for someone who is compatible spiritually, relationally and creatively.

Guidelines for co-writing.

There are no set rules; use constructive not destructive criticism; allow enough time; agree to agree; have a generous heart and keep your purpose in mind.

EXERCISES

1. **Find out how you work best**

   Choose someone who you think could be compatible and set aside two hours to work together on a song. Spend the whole time together and work together on both the music and lyrics. By the end of this time you should have some idea of how you both prefer to work.

2. **Practice critiquing each other's songs**

   Find two or three other songwriters and have a mini

workshop. Each one should play a completed song to the others and ask for feedback. Look at every element of the song from music to lyrics to overall message. Remember to use constructive criticism and do not become defensive about what is said about your song. Work together on the songs and then go away and work as individuals on your own songs before meeting together again. Repeat the process until you feel that you have all improved your songs as much as you want to.

3. Writing either words or music
Find someone who loves to do what you find hard, whether that be the lyrics or the music and pool your skills. This may involve taking pre-composed music and putting lyrics to it or composing a melody for lyrics that have already been written. Discuss any changes that you want to make to your partner's work before making them.

CHAPTER 19

LISTENING TO SONGS

We all stand on the shoulders of giants. Those who have gone before us have carved out new artistic ground that then becomes the starting point for our exploration and creativity.

As you have been reading this book you will have seen how much I have drawn from specific examples to illustrate whatever point I am trying to teach. This is not so that we simply copy what others have done and become clones but so that we can learn from them and then process what we have learned into our own unique expression.

All progress builds from those who have gone before. Most songs are a synthesis of previous styles, chord progressions, melodic lines and lyric ideas with, hopefully, a touch of uniqueness that comes from the composer's individuality.

'Listen to contemporary songs that connect with you. Analyse them, imitate them and then use the principles. Hopefully by that stage it will flow a little bit naturally.' **Reuben Morgan**

KEYS TO GOOD LISTENING

In my experience musicians can be really bad listeners. I have lost count of the times when a musician friend has played me a song that they love and then proceeded to talk throughout it. Now maybe that is because they have already listened carefully to it many times already but I think we can all improve our listening skills.

Listen widely

We have been focussing on songs written for worship but it is a good idea to listen to *good* songs from the full gamut of musical experience. Remember that even though a songwriter may have no religious belief at all, he or she is still made in the image of God and there is some wonderful, inspiring, creative writing going on outside the church that we can learn from. Obviously musically we can gain from doing this but we can also benefit lyrically as we listen to fresh images and powerful language. We need the stimulus of fresh sounds to stretch our writing or we become stale and repetitive. This may include listening to music that you would not normally be interested in.

Even when listening to worship songs we should try to listen widely. Because of the nature of this book I have used examples from songs written by the Hillsong team for the most part but we need also to listen to other great songwriters, both past and present, in the church worldwide.

It is a good idea also to listen to great music from other eras in order to gain insight into how music has developed and where we stand in that great procession of creativity. Listen also to the great old hymns and carols that are still around today and ask why they are still being sung.

'I love listening to orchestral music because you always hear new kinds of sounds in there, new kinds of harmonies that you might not have picked up on the first few listenings. I love what they call "New 20th century" music...Messaien...he has really amazing harmonies and colours and ideas and the way that he puts them together.' **Raymond Badham**

Listen selectively

Most of today's Top 40 will be forgotten in five years. The same is true for worship songs. Although it is beneficial to listen to a wide selection of songs, when you study them in the way that I suggest in the exercises at the end of this chapter pick songs that have already stood the test of time. Life is too short to spend ages listening to a song that really does not have much to it however popular it might be for a couple of weeks. Many of the songs I have used from our own songwriters are ones that have stood the test of time and are still sung regularly around the world. Some are more recent and, although I chose them because they are good examples of specific principles, time will tell whether they have longevity.

Listen intelligently

We tend to be poor listeners often only taking in the beat or the chorus of a song. We all have our favourite aspects of songwriting but we need to broaden that. Musicians need to start listening to the lyrics while lyricists need to start thinking about how the melody is constructed or what is happening in the arrangement. Listen for different elements each time if you want to develop your skills.

Listen wisely

When you are listening to secular music remember that music in itself is amoral, neither good nor bad. However some music, because of the associations it has for you, may not be helpful for you to listen to. The style of music does not make it evil: we judge it by the witness of our spirit. There is always a danger that, if we continually listen to music that we feel uneasy about, we can become desensitized to the whisper of the Holy Spirit. It is possible also to listen to two songs by the same songwriter and to reject one song and yet enjoy another. These are personal decisions but if you are unsure then don't listen because whatever is not of faith is sin. (Romans 14:23)

Obviously, when it comes to lyrics the decision is much clearer. It does not matter how brilliant the music is if the lyric content is promoting sin. Find some equally brilliant music in the style you want to listen to that will not affect your spirit.

SUMMARY

We all learn from those who have gone before and so need to listen to songs as well as write them.

Listen widely
Listen to music of all types and eras in order to increase your musical and lyric vocabulary.

Listen selectively
Be discerning about what you listen to. Popularity does not always equate to quality.

Listen intelligently
Apply your mind to your listening and listen to different elements of the music.

Listen wisely.
Be sensitive to the Holy Spirit in the grey area of what you should not be listening to.

EXERCISES

Choose a worship chorus that you have a recording of and listen to it several times. Each time analyze a different aspect of it. Try to do this without referring to the sheet music, if you have it, so that you develop your listening ability.

1. Song form.
Is it Verse/Chorus? Does it have a Bridge section?

- If the song is in a different form what is it?
- How does the form help the overall communication of the song?

2. Melody.

Is it memorable? Can you hum it back after a couple of hearings?

- Does the melody line move in small steps or large jumps?
- What is the melodic range?
- What are melodic differences between in the different sections?
- How easy would the melody be for a congregation to sing?

3. Lyrics.

Does the song have a message?

- Does the chorus encapsulate the message of the song?
- Do the lyrics state truths about life that you can relate to?
- Does the song use images? How well do they work
- Is rhyme used? If so, how? Is it exact or near rhyme?
- Do the lyrics fit with the rhythm of the music?
- Do the lyrics complement the melody emotionally?
- Are the lyrics contemporary?
- How easily do you think the lyrics could be translated into another language?

4. Harmony.

What chords are being used?

- Do they suit the general feel of the song?
- Does the song rely on the harmony for its feel?
- Are the chords simple or complex?
- Would an inexperienced musician be able to play these harmonies?

5 Rhythm.

- How would you describe the rhythm of the song?
- Does the rhythm place the song firmly in a particular style? If so, what?
- Are the rhythms contemporary in their feel?
- Are they simple or complex?
- Is syncopation used?
- What is the time signature?
- Does the time signature change during the song?
- How easily could an inexperienced musician play these rhythms?

6. Arrangement.

Is there much space in the arrangement or is it very busy?

How many instruments are used and when?

- Is the sound electronic or acoustic in its feel?
- How does the bass line add to the effect of the song?
- Does the bass have its own riffs and melodies or is it purely used for rhythm?
- Is the bass playing the root notes of the chords or inversions?
- Follow another instrument. How does it fit in the overall arrangement?
- What does it add to the song?
- Could this arrangement be played by an inexperienced band in a small church?

CHAPTER 20

THE BUSINESS OF SONGWRITING

By Steve McPherson - CEO, Hillsong Music Publishing

T he business of song writing can be a confusing world, but it is crucial for today's song writers to understand the basics in order for them to see the full potential of their writing realised. In these next few pages I will give you a quick summary on some of the areas that you should be aware of.

COPYRIGHT

Copyright is really not as scary as it sounds. It is basically the rights held by a creator of a work whether that is literary, dramatic, musical or an artistic work, irrespective of quality.

As the writer of a song, the exclusive rights under the copyright of that song that are held by you are:

1. The right to reproduce the <u>work</u> in a <u>material form</u>. This could be an audio and/or a visual recording of the song. (Known as the "mechanical right")

2. The right to synchronise the work with another media, i.e. film, videos and multimedia. (Known as the "synchronisation right")

3. The right to publish or print the <u>work</u>. That is, any print reproductions whether it is lyrics sheet or full sheet music.

4. The right to perform or communicate the <u>work</u> in public.

5. The right to <u>broadcast</u> the <u>work</u> on television, radio or the internet.

6. The right to make a secondary work from the original song. This includes musical arrangements and translations.

7. The right to reproduce, publish, perform or broadcast the secondary work, as mentioned in number 5.

8. The right to sell the work in any format.

As the owner of the copyright, YOU are the only person permitted by law carry out the above-mentioned activities; anyone else must seek your permission first. Copyright law does change from country to country, however the basic rights do remain the same worldwide.

These rights remain yours unless you assign or license them to a third party. Typically, this is where a music publisher comes in. In order for them to do their job of administering and promoting your song, they need to contractually own or control the copyright on your behalf. *(See section on publishers)*

Licensing

Licensing is the process by which people gain permission to use songs. If you have not assigned your rights to a publisher and your songs are being heard, then you may need to consider a licensing plan. When people start to use your songs, there is a small amount of administration that goes along with this. Keep it simple. But establish a procedure for this that you can use to grant people permission when they request it.

Co-writing

When a song is co-written by more than one author, the copyright ownership in the song is shared. It is important that the percentage share of the ownership is agreed upon either before writing or upon completion of the song. There are a few approaches used to determine the share of a song, including;

- *Equal shares (the "Nashville" method).* When two or more writers get together to write a song, they will often agree to even shares before they begin writing, regardless of the level of participation of each writer present, whether that be regarding music, melody or lyrics. This alleviates any disagreements on everyone's participation.
- *Who did what?* Determining the share of the song based on the level of participation of each writer. Who had the initial idea? Who did the most work? Whose ideas are the most significant and important ideas to the song?
- *50% for lyrics, 50% for music.* If you are going to split the song by the level of participation of each writer, a good place to start is by separating the lyrics and music, giving a 50% share to each. Lyrics being purely the literary work of song and music being any melodic or harmonic idea that is either sung or played by an instrument that is significant to the song. Because it can be difficult to determine what is and isn't a significant musical idea, a good rule of thumb is to ask if the idea can be separated from the song. Does the song still work without this musical idea? An example is a guitar riff – is it synonymous with the song or does the song live without it? It is worth noting that this method can

be problematic as it raises questions surrounding the value of a contribution or musical element.

Whichever method is utilized to determine the split, once it is agreed, get it in writing so that it is clear to everyone and can be referred to in the future.

Piracy

Just as there is a copyright protection in your material, be aware of the rights of other writers. It is very important that song writers are careful not to illegally use other people's material. A melody, or riff, or even a chord progression is a part of the overall copyright of the song, and therefore is owned by the writers or assigned owner of that work.

It is a good habit to get into to keep all your working notes for your song, as proof that your work is in fact, your work.

Copyright Registration

This is an area that is quite often confused. Some countries require copyright owners to register their works to confirm copyright ownership, the USA being one of those countries. In the USA, all copyrights (whether musical, dramatic, artistic or literary) are registered at the Library of Congress in Washington DC.

In Australia there is no registration process. According to Australian Copyright Law, copyright is, by default, owned by the author and is protected by Copyright law at the point in time when the work becomes tangible. i.e. Print or recording.

Song titles do not need to be registered on their own as there is no copyright to a title, unless it is trademarked, and there is a similar, but separate process for this

MUSIC PUBLISHERS

The function of a music publisher:
1. Publish sheet music or license others to publish it
2. Persuade artists and record companies to record the copyright,
3. Promote music to potential users, such as film and TV producers. Negotiating respective licensing agreements.
4. Collect fees and royalties earned for the commissioning or exploitation of music.
5. Promoting the reputation of their writers.
6. Protecting the works from unauthorised use.
7. Administration, i.e. registration, maintaining and protecting copyrights.

Contracts

When looking at a publishing contract always seek advice from someone experienced in music publishing or make contact with an entertainment lawyer. There are a lot of complexities in a publishing contract, and this needs to be taken seriously.

Types of music publishing contract

- *Writer for Hire Agreements* - Companies employing writers to compose music. Normally in this case the publisher owns the copyright, but it would depend on the agreement.
- *Single Song Assignments* - This is where a publisher, only takes on a single song or selected group of songs. The copyright is transferred to this company for an allocated period.
- *Term Publishing Agreements* - Where a publisher takes full control of your all your material for the term of the agreements. Including material written prior to the agreements and written during the agreement.

- **Self-Publishing** - Many writers choose to set up their own publishing house, and retain their copyrights and publisher royalties.
- **Administration Deals** - This is where the publisher simply takes the administration work of protecting copyrights and collecting royalties for the composer, but the composer retains the actual copyrights and is solely responsible for the promotion of the copyrights.

ROYALTIES

Different type of royalties received by song writers:
1. Mechanical royalties – from the sale of recorded product, either physical or digital.
2. Print royalties – from the sale of sheet music, or other items containing printed lyrics.
3. Synchronisation royalties – fees received from synchronization licenses.
4. Performance royalties – royalties received form performance rights organisation (PRO) for live performances, radio airplay, television broadcast or online streaming.
5. Church licensing royalties – royalties received from church licensing organisations such as CCLI.

To receive royalties for the reproduction of your songs is your right, and you should never be forced to waive that right, however many song writers redirect their royalties to churches, or charities. This is your choice and your choice alone.
- **Mechanical royalties** Mechanical royalties are calculated differently in every country. Some countries use a percentage rate based on either the recommended retail price or the wholesale

price of the product being sold. However, the United States, for example use a cent rate for each song. The mechanical rates do change periodically, but are usually set by a statutory body or determined through industry consultation and negotiation. Mechanical rates for digital reproductions differ from those of physical products.

- **Print royalties** Generally paid at a percentage rate of the retail price of the music book or sheet music. This rate can vary depending on the extent of the arrangement or the type of sheet music being sold. For merchandise items such as t-shirts or artwork containing lyrics, this is also a percentage of the retail price of the item.

- **Synchronisation royalties** Unlike mechanical royalties, synchronisation fees are purely negotiable and are not regulated. Fees can vary as low as free for an unknown and un-released songs for a local public TV program, up to $250,000 or more for a major artist's hit song featured in a high-budget feature film. Generally, however, synchronisation fees are determined and negotiated based on a number of objective and subjective factors.

- **Performance royalties** Performance royalties are paid by the performance rights organisation (PRO) in each territory, and are generally paid separately to both the song writer and the publisher. However, if you are not signed to a publisher, you should be receiving this in full. The PRO's deduct from gross receipts a small administrative fee.

- **Church Licensing royalties** Song writers who write for church worship have the potential to earn royalties from licensing organisations who license the reproduction of music for worship usage, and pay song writers and publishers a royalty based on the revenue collected. (*see further information below*)

COLLECTION AGENCIES

A collection agency specifies a particular right or group of rights within a copyright, and licences a particular market on behalf of the copyright holders, whether that is the writer or the representing publisher or publishers.

Performance Rights Organisations (PRO)

There are PROs in most nations of the world today, licensing and collecting revenue on behalf of song writers and publishers for the live performance, and broadcast rights. Here are a just a few of the PRO's around the world.

APRA – (Australia)
[www.apraamcos.com.au]

ASCAP – Publishers (USA)
[www.ascap.com]

BMI - (USA)
[www.bmi.com]

SESAC – (USA)
[www.sesac.co]

PRS - (UK)
[www.prs.co.uk]

SOCAN – (Canada)
[www.socan.ca]

Mechanical Rights Organisations

There are also organisations that license and collect specifically the mechanical right on behalf of copyright owners. A lot of the PRO's around the world, do also license mechanical reproduction, but there are stand alone companies that only license mechanical rights, such as:

The Harry Fox Agency, Inc (USA)
[www.harryfox.com]

MCPS (UK)
[www.mcps.co.uk]

AMCOS – (Australia)
[www.amcos.com.au]

Church Licensing Organisations

These organisations license the church for the reproduction of songs specifically for church use.

CCLI
[www.ccli.com]

OneLicense
[www.onelicense.net)

Suggested websites

Australian Copyright Council
[www.copyright.org.au]

US Copyright Office
[www.copyright.gov]

MusicContracts.com
[www.musiccontracts.com]

National Music Publishers' Association (NMPA)
[www.nmpa.org]

AFTERWORD: IT'S NOT ABOUT ME!

I want to finish by considering this question one last time. Why do we write songs for worship? I think there are four statements that we would do well to bear in mind.

It's not about me, well it's a little bit about me!

It is not about my fame or glory. It is not about being recognised as an amazing songwriter or getting my songs on albums but it **is** about me in that my songs need to be authentic. They need to express a genuine faith and to reflect who I am as a songwriter. There's no point in trying to be a Joel Houston or a Darlene Zschech. God does not need any copies. My calling is to bring what only I can uniquely bring.

It's not about me, it's about Him

Our worship songs are both addressed to God and are about Him and we need to be careful about both these elements. If He is not being exalted in our songs then we are just singing songs and not worshipping. And if we are writing about God in a way that distorts the truth about Him then we are not worshipping the true God and that is idolatry.

It's not about me, it's about us

Once we have sorted out that we need to be authentic but not self-focussed and that our purpose is to worship God in Spirit and Truth then we have to consider who will be singing our songs. First and foremost that will be our local congregation whether it is in the youth group, an extension service or a campus service. Are we writing well for our community?

It's not about me, it's about them

Some of our songs may have a life beyond our local church. They may end up on albums and they may be sung globally. Are we writing for those people who we may never meet but whose worship is going to be influenced by our songs? This is a huge responsibility. Am I writing lyrics that can relate to any culture or generation? Am I writing songs that have the potential to last?

It is only appropriate to finish by revisiting what I quoted at the start of this book and that encapsulates so much of what this book has sought to facilitate.

'The church that I see is a worshipping church whose songs reflect such a passion for Christ that others sense His magnificence and power. A distinct sound that emanates from a healthy church, contagious in spirit – creating music that resounds from villages and tribes to great cities and nations.' Brian Houston – The church that I now see

APPENDIX A:
THE MAJOR THEMES
IN THE PSALMS

———

'Awake, O Lord! Why do you sleep?
Rouse yourself! Do not reject us forever.
Why do you hide your face
and forget our misery and oppression?
(PSALM 44:23,24 NIV)

———

What are the themes of worship? What is suitable subject matter when we are addressing God? Are there things that we should not say to him? When we look at the book of Psalms we see that the psalmists expressed the whole gamut of emotional responses from joy and thanksgiving to anger and despair. Worship in the psalms included every situation that we face as human beings from sickness and grief to celebration and triumph and everything in between. The message of the psalms is that, if we experience it, then we can and should talk to God about it.

We may feel that asking God why he appears to have forgotten us (Psalm 13) or calling for vengeance on our enemies (Psalm 109) or crying out in despair (Psalm 88) are inappropriate ways to address God. However God, in His sovereignty, has allowed these expressions of what seem to us less than positive attitudes to become part of the Bible. Perhaps He wants us to learn something from these worshippers.

Clearly some of the ways in which we worship have changed in the light of the death and resurrection of Jesus Christ but we must be careful not to throw out all what we can learn from the psalms and their subject matter simply because we see them as old covenant. After all, the Old Testament was Jesus' Bible and the psalms were the songs that Jesus would have sung in the synagogue week by week and that He quoted from on a number of occasions.

So what can we learn from the psalms as songwriters?

'I think in every way the Psalms are gradually shaping my songwriting because hopefully they are shaping me.'
Reuben Morgan

THE PSALMS REFLECT THE DIFFERENT SEASONS OF LIFE

One of the great themes of literature and of life is that of home, discovery and return. You only have to read 'The Odyssey' by Homer, 'Lord of the Rings' by JRR Tolkein, or the stories of the Prodigal son or Jacob to see this theme worked out. Home represents security and everything that is worth fighting for. Then events, either external or internal, cause the protagonist in the story to set out on a journey of discovery where he is tested. Throughout the journey however he retains a sense of home that is often contrasted to what he is experiencing now. Finally he returns home again changed by what he has been through and passes on what he has learned to the next generation (Psalm 78).

Jesus' life reflects this theme. He left His home in heaven, prompted by love for us, to undertake a dangerous, sacrificial journey of discovery. He experienced everything that we experience as humanity. Ultimately that took Him to the cross. In a turnaround that could only be of divine origin, He triumphed over death and returned to His heavenly home with a name that is above all names.

This theme of home, discovery and return needs words to accompany it however. It is through words that we express and make sense of the events of our life. And that is where the psalms come in. In the psalms the writers speak to God of what is going on in their lives and of the different seasons that they are in. These seasons which can be either personal or communal may occur more than once in a person or community's life.

For the rest of the chapter I am going to look at various types of psalms that fall into these three themes of home, discovery and return which are loosely based on Walter Breuggemann's categories in his book 'The Message of the Psalms.[24] You may disagree with some of the categories I have used or even over which psalm fits into which category but I am only trying to give a rough guide to a huge subject. I have also made suggestions about how each type could be used by a Christian songwriter today.

SONGS OF HOME
(The settled season)

The psalms that fit into this category all have in common a confidence in God's reliability and sovereignty. The writers of the Psalms were in covenant relationship with their God and trusted that, as they kept His commands, He would bless and protect them. As Christians we can identify with this season. This season is one when we enjoy the blessing of God; when we have no challenges

---

24 Walter Brueggemann *The Message of the Psalms* Augsbury, Minneapolis USA 1984

that are testing our faith to its limits; when we see that living according to God's Word works and when we have a general sense of wellbeing and gratitude to a God Who is clearly present and active in our world. Our confidence is based on our covenant relationship with God through Christ.

These psalms can loosely be grouped into three categories:

Songs of the King: Royal and Enthronement psalms

Royal psalms Examples include psalms 2, 18, 20, 21, 45, 72, 110, 132)

———

*'The Lord says to my Lord: "Sit at my right hand
until I make your enemies a footstool for your feet."'*
(PSALM 110:1 NIV)

———

The royal psalms are psalms in which the king plays a part. Originally they would have referred to a reigning king but, with the fall of Jerusalem and the failing of the monarchy, they came to be understood as referring to a future king and acquired a messianic tone.

Christian songwriters. In these psalms we find prophetic references to Jesus and beautiful imagery about royalty in general that can be adapted to relate to our worship of the King of kings.

Enthronement psalms Examples include psalms 47,93, 96-99)

———

*'The Lord reigns, let the earth be glad;
Let the distant shores rejoice.'*
(PSALM 97:1 NIV)

———

God is praised in these psalms for His majesty and rule that extends beyond the borders of Israel to include the whole world. In looking at God's reign there is also an element of His future judgment in these psalms.

Christian songwriters. These songs focus on God's sovereignty and rule and can be great songs that both express and build faith in those who sing them. As Christians we understand that the promise to Abraham has been fulfilled in Christ and is being fulfilled as the gospel is preached throughout the world.

Songs of commitment: Wisdom/Torah psalms

Examples include psalms 1, 19, 34, 37, 49, 73, 112, 119, 127)

———

'Your word is a lamp to my feet
and a light to my path.'
(PSALM 119:105 NIV)

———

The laws of the Old Testament spring from the covenant relationship between Israel and a holy God and those who keep them are blessed. When we read the wisdom psalms it is apparent that the writers delighted in the divine order represented by the law and it is compared to honey or treasure (Psalm 1:10). The law was the guide to right living and it was righteous because God is righteous. As in the New Testament, keeping God's commands came as a response to grace and redemption rather than a means of earning it (Exodus 19:4,5).

Christian songwriters As Christians we tend to read these psalms in relation to the Bible rather than the law specifically and writing songs that delight in God's word are valid expressions of worship.

Songs of wonder: Descriptive praise and creation psalms

Descriptive praise psalms Examples include psalms 29, 33, 100, 103, 117, 134-136, 139, 145-150)

_____

'Praise the Lord,
Praise God in his sanctuary;
praise him in his mighty heavens.'
(Psalm 150:1 NIV)

_____

These songs praise God for who He is and what He does and could equally well fit into the new settled season category.

Christian songwriters This is an ideal theme for us as worshippers and needs no   further explanation.

Creation psalms Examples include psalms 8,19a, 104,139)

_____

'O Lord, our Lord, how majestic is your name in all the earth!'
(PSALM 8:1 NIV)

_____

Creation psalms praise the Creator who has ordered the world and continues to rule over and sustain it. Creation reminds man of his purpose (Psalm 8:3-8; 139:13f) and inspires a sense of wonder and deep gratitude to the God who cares so deeply for us.

Christian songwriters. There is such a wealth of material in creation and God's part in it to inspire us as songwriters. The fact that we know more about how it works scientifically than the writers of the psalms did simply causes us to be more amazed at our endlessly creative God.

SONGS OF DISCOVERY
(*The unsettled season*)

So many things could turn a settled season into an unsettled one for the writers of the Psalms. As a community they faced the threat of war or drought or famine. As individuals they faced personal attack, sickness, betrayal, the results of sin and even death. Things are not so different for us today. Life can go along smoothly and then suddenly something happens and we face challenges that can threaten to derail us. Our faith is shaken by events that we feel should not be happening to us as Christians. These challenges can range from losing a job to a marriage breakdown, serious sickness or bereavement. Even less extreme events such as going to college, changing city or starting a family can bring challenges and questions. But as we go through the challenge with God, as the writers of the psalms did in the laments, this season can be a time of discovery and growth.

Songs of anguish - Laments

There are about 50 individual laments in the book of Psalms including psalms 3-7, 10-14, 22, 25, 26, 28, 54-57, 59, 61, 64, 69, 73, 88, 109, 140-143. Communal laments include Psalms 12, 44, 60, 74, 79, 80, 83, 85, 89)

———

'How long, Lord? Will you forget me forever?
How long will you hide your face from me?
(PSALM 13:1 NIV)

———

These songs, prompted by situations of crisis, express a deep trust in God as the writer brings his times of darkness and despair to Him in all the rawness of emotion that accompanies that.

Christian songwriters. It is hard to imagine a regular place for the lament in our worship although the laments form part of the worship of some churches. Because of what Jesus has done we have a hope that extends beyond death and understand that ultimately nothing can separate us from God whereas, for the writers of the psalms, God's deliverance had to be decided in the petitioner's lifetime. However acknowledging the reality of a painful situation is not a lack of faith when we recognise that God is present and listening in dark times too. So, while there may be no place for an individual song of lament in our corporate worship, there is a place for such songs in our personal lives that, in another context, may help others to find words for their dark times just as the psalms have helped so many people over the years.

In addition, there is possibly a place for communal lament when the church joins together to address God about a situation that concerns us all.

'Honesty. That's the biggest blessing I get from the psalms. I guess predominately the thought that it's alright to tell God exactly how you feel and not just what people may tell you to say.' **Marty Sampson**

Songs of trust

Examples include psalms 11, 16, 23,27, 63, 71, 91, 121, 131)

'I lift up my eyes to the hills - where does my help come from? My help comes from the Lord, the Maker of heaven and earth.'
(PSALM 121:1 NIV)

These songs are all expressions of trust in the presence of threat. They are less intense than the lament in that, although the threat is still present, they are slightly distanced from the specific event and speak of God as being trustworthy in the face of any threat that might come against them. There is a certainty about these songs that is often absent in the desperation of the lament.

Christian songwriters. These psalms are much loved by Christians and are probably among the most familiar and frequently set psalms in the whole book. Their themes of confidence in God in the face of difficulty work well in contemporary worship.

SONGS OF RETURN
(*The new settled season*)

This concept of the unexpected turnaround, when events had seemed to be hopeless and to be going so badly, inspired Tolkein to coin the word 'eucatastrophe'. Eucatastrophe expresses the sudden change of fortunes that leads to a happy ending. For Christians it describes the joy of the resurrection after the despair of the cross but it could also be used to describe what happens in many of the psalms when, against all the odds, God turns up and everything changes.

Songs of gratitude - Thanksgiving psalms

Examples include psalms 9, 18, 30, 40 ,92, 116, 138 with psalms 107, 124 and 129 as examples of communal thanksgiving psalms.

———

'I will exalt you, O Lord,
for you lifted me out of the depths
and did not let my enemies gloat over me.'
(PSALM 30:1 NIV)

———

These songs are a response to grace and they flow out of the laments. Every thanksgiving psalm is well aware of a recent need that has now been met by God. As a result the language is one of gratitude and amazement at the change in circumstances.

Christian songwriter Whenever Christians sing of their salvation they sing a thanksgiving psalm. The challenge is to write a song that is not so personal and specific that it cannot be sung by anyone else. Other causes for thanksgiving may include physical and emotional healing, rescue from spiritual enemies, God's provision and many other situations. Songs that remind us of where we have come from are a vital part of our worship and, hopefully, stop us from ever becoming familiar with the goodness of God.

Songs of victory - Narrative praise psalms

Examples include psalms 78, 105, 106, 114, 135, 136)

———

'O my people, hear my teaching
listen to the words of my mouth.
I will open my mouth in parables,
I will utter hidden things, things from of old'
(PSALM 78:1,2 NIV)

———

In some ways these psalms fit into both the settled and new settled seasons as they look back at great events in Israel's history where God has shown himself to be faithful to his covenant promises. These psalms retell the event in order to encourage future generations to trust and praise God.

Christian songwriters. Our great event that we sing about for the generations to come is the death and resurrection of the Lord Jesus Christ. We will never tire of telling and retelling the story of what He has done for us and of the new covenant that has been established by His blood. Luke 1:69-79 and Philippians 2:6-12 are New Testament examples of narrative psalms.

'Psalm 18 was a psalm I have loved, memorized and meditated on day and night. I loved lines in it such as "by you I can run against a troop; with my God, I can leap over a wall!" Often I have felt ill-prepared for what life has brought my way, but the greatest obstacles aren't a problem to him! I simply get Go-go Inspector Gadget legs and jump the wall of every corner the enemy backs me into.' **Tanya Riches**

SUMMARY

The Psalms show us what is suitable subject matter to bring before God.

The Psalms reflect the different seasons of life.
They cover the move from a settled to unsettled season and the move out of that season to a new season of gratitude for God's deliverance.

Songs of Home
These include royal, enthronement, wisdom, creation and descriptive praise psalms all of which are appropriate themes for us as worship songwriters.

Songs of Discovery

These include laments and songs of trust. Laments are best suited to our personal journey but songs of trust work well in corporate worship.

Songs of Return

These include thanksgiving and narrative praise psalms both of which are suited to corporate worship.

EXERCISES

1. **Songs of Home**

   Read a psalm from one of the categories described in this season and use it as the basis for a song lyric that would be suitable for corporate worship.

2. **Songs of Discovery**

   Read some of the songs of trust and write your own. Use your own experience of challenge and the confidence that you found in God then to bring your authenticity to the song but remember to keep it general enough to be sung by a congregation.

3. **Songs of Return**

   Write a lyric of exuberant thankfulness for something that God has done in your life. In your first draft do not worry too much about how specific you are being, simply focus on the emotion behind the experience. Then, when you revise your lyric, make sure that it can be sung by a congregation.

APPENDIX B:
HEBREW PARALLELISM

———

'Praise the Lord, O my soul;
all my inmost being, praise his holy name.'
(PSALM 103:1 NIV)

———

Have you ever noticed how the writers of the psalms seem to repeat themselves? They make a statement such as 'Praise the Lord, O my soul' and in the very next line seem to say something almost identical.   And it is not just the writers of the psalms who do that. Whenever we find poetry or poetic expressions in the Bible the same thing happens whether it is in the prophetic books:

———

'Does a lion roar in the thicket when he has no prey?
Does he growl in his den when he has caught nothing?'
(AMOS 3:4 NIV)

———

Or in the book of Proverbs:

———

'Listen, my son, to your father's instruction
and do not forsake your mother's teaching.
They will be a garland to grace your head
and a chain to adorn your neck.'
(PROVERBS 1:8,9 NIV)

———

Even Jesus did it!

———

'Which of you, if his son asks for bread, will give him a stone?
Or if he asks for a fish, will give him a snake?'
(MATTHEW 7:9 NIV)

———

So what is happening here and what does it have to do with us as songwriters? I believe that parallelism is a powerful poetic and communicative device that we can use in our songwriting to great effect. Hopefully you will be as enthusiastic about it by the end of the chapter as I am.

WHAT IS PARALLELISM?

There have been hundreds of books written both on the Psalms and on Hebrew poetry so all I want to do here is sketch the outline of a big subject. For further reading I would recommend 'How to Read the Psalms' by Tremper Longman III[25]. This is a good introduction to the psalms written in layman's terms.

Parallelism defined

A fundamental characteristic of Hebrew poetry is the way it tends to echo one thought with another as I have illustrated at the start of this chapter. Perhaps the easiest way to explain what is going on is to use the example of the way our eyes work and how that affects the way we see the world. If you cover up one eye you can see everything perfectly clearly but what you cannot judge accurately is depth. In order to see that you need to use both eyes and the two slightly different views of the same object that are sent to your brain give you the sense of depth.

———

25   Tremper Longman III *How to Read the Psalms* IVP 1988 UK

Scholars, particularly James Kugel, became aware that the same sort of process was happening when the poets used parallelism. The parallel line was not exactly the same as the first line but was adding something to the first thought and so adding depth to what was being said. When we read Hebrew poetry and come across parallel constructions

we are not intended to reduce the two lines to one statement but to read the first and then look for what is added to our understanding in the second.

e.g. 'The heavens declare the glory of God;

the skies proclaim the work of his hands.' (Psalm 19:1 NIV)

The first line contains the picture of creation expressing God's glory. The second line takes that thought further by stating that part of what we understand in God's glory is His creation, more specifically, the work of His hands.

Different types of parallelism

There are various theories in scholarly circles about how to categorise the different types of parallelism and I have not included a full list but only what I think could be of interest to us as songwriters. I have based this list on the one in Tremper Longman's 'How to Read the Psalms.'

Synonymous parallelism The same thought is repeated using different but closely related sets of words that take us a little further.

e.g. 'He does not treat us as our sins deserve

or repay us according to our iniquities.' (Psalm 103:10 NIV)

Note here that the 2nd line brings in the concept of repayment which has stronger connotations than 'treat'. It implies that our sins would normally always result in action on God's part.

Antithetic parallelism The same thought is repeated in different words but using antonyms (e.g. short/tall) instead of synonyms. What is happening here is that the same thought is being expressed from different perspectives and this is what adds depth. We see both the positive and negative sides.

e.g. 'Hatred stirs up dissension,

but love covers over all wrongs.' (Proverbs 10:12 NIV)

e.g. 'Some trust in chariots and some in horses,

but we trust in the name of the Lord our God.' (Psalm 20:7 NIV)

e.g. 'He has filled the hungry with good things

but has sent the rich away empty.' (Luke 1:53 NIV)

Emblematic parallelism This uses analogy and comparisons to bring thoughts from different areas of life together.

e.g. 'As the deer pants for streams of water,

so my soul pants for you, O God.' (Psalm 42:1 NIV)

Here a deer suffering from natural thirst is compared to our souls thirsting for God.

Step parallelism (repetitive, climactic) The first statement is partially repeated but carried further in second and third lines.

e.g.

———

> 'Ascribe to the Lord, O mighty ones,
> ascribe to the Lord glory and strength.
> Ascribe to the Lord the glory due his name;'
> (PSALM 29:1,2 NIV)

———

Notice how the repetition of the phrase 'ascribe to the Lord' has a new element added to it on each repetition. In the second line we learn what it is that we are to ascribe to the Lord and in the third line we learn why we should ascribe glory to Him. So each line builds from the other. I find it helpful to ask questions of each line in order to see what has been added.

Chiasm A chiasm is so named because the Greek letter Chi looks like an X. In this version of parallelism the second line reverses the order of units found in the first line.

e.g.

———

'**I will declare your name** *to my brothers;*
in the congregation **I will praise you.**'
(PSALM 22:22 NIV)

———

If we break each of these lines down into two phrases we find that the phrase in bold print, **'I will declare your name,'** at the start of line 1 complements, **'I will praise you,'** at the end of line 2. In the same way the phrase, 'to my brothers,' at the end of line 1 complements the phrase, 'in the congregation,' at the start of line 2.   If you draw a line from each of the phrases in the first line to their comparable phrases in the 2nd line you end up with the shape of a Chi (X).

e.g.

———

'**Do not give dogs** *what is sacred;*
do not throw your pearls **to pigs**'
(MATTHEW 7:6 NIV)

———

e.g.

———

'**Praise the Lord**, *O my soul;*
all my inmost being, **praise his holy name.**'
(PSALM 103:1 NIV)

———

WHY USE PARALLELISM IN CONTEMPORARY SONGWRITING?

If you have stayed with me so far in this brief discussion of parallelism you may still be wondering what place it has in a book on songwriting. Let me give you a few suggestions and I will include a few examples that I have found in contemporary songs. I am not sure if the writers necessarily always realised what they were doing but, if you live in the poetry of the Bible for long enough, some things tend to rub off on you.

Parallelism was the poetic device that God chose to use in the Bible

The significant thing about Hebrew poetry is that it depends for its beauty and impact, not so much on the sound of the words, but on the meaning of the words. Hebrew poetry's use of parallelism and lack of emphasis on rhythm or rhyme set it apart from many of the poems and lyrics that we read today.

However increasingly there has been a move away from rhyme and regular metre in modern poetry and song lyrics which has left the way open for other method of creating repetition and rhythm in the words. Parallelism is one such method and God chose to inspire his writers to use it consistently throughout the Bible which makes me stop and think about whether it has something to say to me today as a writer.

e.g.

———

'King of Majesty' (Marty Sampson)

'These words are from my heart
These words are not made up.'

———

The 2nd line stresses the genuineness of these words that are being sung. They are not simply any old words to fill up a line but they are heartfelt words.

Parallelism helps to solve problems of translation

One of the problems of having our songs sung in other countries is that of translation. If you translate every word exactly you lose the rhythm and stresses of the original lyric and can end up with something that just does not work with the music. If the original lyrics were heavily dependent on rhyme and clever plays on words all of that will be lost once they are translated because the beauty of the lyrics was found in the sound rather than the sense.

But parallelism relies not on sound but on what is being said and that can be translated into any language without losing its effect. It is now not a question of finding particular rhymes or words but simply of repeating the concept of the parallel construction and what it means. That will make the translator's job easier.

When I first considered this in relation to the poetry of the Bible I found it so moving to realise that God in His wisdom and foreknowledge had inspired the biblical poets to write poetry that could be translated into any language in any age and that would retain its distinctive beauty because it was about the meaning rather than the sound. The poets' use of images and parallelism transcends every age.

e.g.

———

'Through It All' (Reuben Morgan)

'You are forever in my life
You see me through the seasons'

———

Line 1 speaks of God's presence in a life while line 2 adds depth to the first statement by considering that a life has different seasons.

———

'And I look to you
And I wait on you'

———

The 'look' in line 1 has become more specific in the next line as the singer speaks of waiting on God.

Parallelism is a great communication device

This use of repetition that adds something in the repeated line is a great way of communicating. Every teacher or preacher is aware that saying something once is rarely enough but that important statements need to be reinforced. That is why we say our most important things in the choruses of our songs so that we can repeat them. This device helps us to do that even more effectively because the repetitions are not exactly the same and therefore add something to our understanding each time.

e.g.

———

'You Are' (Darlene Zschech)

'You are my light and salvation whom shall I fear
You are the strength of all my days of whom shall I be afraid'

———

These parallels are drawn straight from the first verse of Psalm 27 but Darlene has chosen to keep the construction rather than trying to make a rhyme out of it.

———

'I will bless the Lord forever
I'll bless Your holy Name.'

———

In the chorus Darlene has continued the parallelism by taking the general 'bless the Lord' in line 1 and becoming more specific in line 2 as we sing about blessing His holy Name.

Parallelism helps with lyric rhythm and takes the pressure off rhyming

Parallelism carries its own rhythms in its repetitions and, because we have already understood that the lines are in pairs, rhyming is less necessary.

A lovely contemporary example of the use of parallelism is found in the first verse of the song 'Blessed Be Your Name' which is also a great example of a song of trust.

———

'Blessed be your name in the land that is plentiful
Where your streams of abundance flow
Blessed be your name
And blessed be your name when I'm found in the desert place
Though I walk through the wilderness
Blessed be your name.'

('BLESSED BE YOUR NAME' BY BETH AND
MATT REDMAN ©2002 THANKYOU MUSIC)

———

Line 2 builds on line 1 by using a specific image to describe a plentiful land. Line 5 builds on line 4 by developing the thought of being found in the desert to walking through it. Notice also that the songwriters have used chiasms.

SUMMARY

Parallelism is used throughout the poetry in the Bible.

What is parallelism?
Parallelism is a way of echoing one thought with another in such a way that depth is added to the original thought. Different types of parallelism include synonymous, antithetic, emblematic, step parallelism and chiasms.

Why use parallelism in contemporary songwriting?
It is the way God chose to inspire the Biblical writers; it helps to solve the problems of translation; it is a great communicative device; it helps with lyric rhythm and takes the pressure off rhyming

EXERCISES

1. Writing parallel constructions.
- Write a line that is an example of synonymous parallelism to the line below:

  ―――

  'Thank you Lord that you heard my cry for mercy'

  ―――

- Write a line that is an example of antithetic parallelism to the line below:

  ―――

  'My enemy had pushed me down

  ―――

But....

- Write a two more lines to create an example of step
  parallelism. Remember to ask questions of each line in
  order to build through the thought.

  _____

  'My heart is lifted up'

  _____

- Write a chiasm that reverses the order of the phrases in the
  line below without using exactly the same words.

  _____

  'I will sing Lord of all you have done'

  _____

2. Write a chorus that uses parallelism

Write a chorus to a worship song and use parallelism rather
than rhyme to link the lines and thoughts together.

APPENDIX C:
LIST OF SONG REFERENCES

Hillsong Songs

Aftermath
Chapter 10
Joel Houston
© 2010 Hillsong Music Publishing
Recorded on Aftermath © Hillsong Music Australia

Alive
Chapters 12, 13, 15, 16
Aodhan King, Alexander Pappas
© 2013 Hillsong Music Publishing
Recorded on We Are Young And Free © Hillsong Music Australia

All I Need Is You
Chapter 15
Marty Sampson
© 2004 Hillsong Music Publishing
Recorded on Look To You © Hillsong Music Australia

Anchor
Chapter 8
Ben Fielding, Dean Ussher
© 2012 Hillsong Music Publishing
Recorded on Glorious Ruins © Hillsong Music Australia

As It Is (In Heaven)
Chapter 16
Joel Houston, Ben Fielding
© 2016 Hillsong Music Publishing
Recorded on Let There Be Light © Hillsong Music Australia

Beneath The Waters (I Will Rise)
Chapters 5, 8
Brooke Ligertwood, Scott Ligertwood
© 2012 Hillsong Music Publishing
Recorded on Cornerstone © Hillsong Music Australia

Broken Vessels (Amazing Grace)
Chapters 5, 10, 14
Joel Houston, Jonas Myrin

© 2014 Hillsong Music Publishing
Recorded on No Other Name © Hillsong Music Australia

Behold (Then Sings My Soul)
Chapter 13
Joel Houston
© 2016 Hillsong Music Publishing
Recorded on Let There Be Light © Hillsong Music Australia

Calvary
Chapter 13
Reuben Morgan, Jonas Myrin, Mrs. Walter G. Taylor
© 2014 Hillsong Music Publishing
Recorded on No Other Name © Hillsong Music Australia

Captain
Chapters 8, 10, 14, 16
Benjamin Hastings, Seth Simmons
© 2014 Hillsong Music Publishing
Recorded on Empires © Hillsong Music Australia

Christ Is Enough
Chapters 5, 14
Reuben Morgan, Jonas Myrin
© 2012 Hillsong Music Publishing
Recorded on Glorious Ruins © Hillsong Music Australia

Cornerstone
Chapters 4, 12, 15, 18
Jonas Myrin, Eric Liljero, Reuben Morgan© 2011 Hillsong Music Publishing
Recorded on Cornerstone © Hillsong Music Australia

Crowns
Chapter 8
Michael Fatkin, Scott Groom, Benjamin Hastings
© 2016 Hillsong Music Publishing
Recorded on Let There Be Light © Hillsong Music Australia

Desert Song
Chapter 8
Brooke Ligertwood
© 2008 Sony/ATV Music Publishing Australia (AUS & NZ only) Hillsong Music
Publishing (Rest of world)
Recorded on Across The Earth © Hillsong Music Australia

Elohim
Chapters 13, 14
Marty Sampson
© 2016 Hillsong Music Publishing
Recorded on Let There Be Light © Hillsong Music Australia

Emmanuel
Chapter 8
Raymond Badham
© 2000 Hillsong Music Publishing
Recorded on You Are My World © Hillsong Music Australia

Empires
Chapters 8, 10, 16
Joel Houston, Dylan Thomas, Chris Davenport, Ben Tennikoff
© 2015 Hillsong Music Publishing
Recorded on Empires © Hillsong Music Australia

Even When It Hurts
Chapter 8
Joel Houston
© 2015 Hillsong Music Publishing
Recorded on Empires © Hillsong Music Australia

Ever Living God
Chapter 12
Raymond Badham
© 2002 Hillsong Music Publishing
Recorded on Hope © Hillsong Music Australia

Forever And A Day
Chapter 11
Raymond Badham
© 2003 Hillsong Music Publishing
Recorded on For All You've Done © Hillsong Music Australia

Gift Of Love
Chapters 8, 11
Amanda Fergusson
© 2004 Hillsong Music Publishing
Recorded on Songs For Communion © Hillsong Music Australia

Glorify Your Name
Chapter 15
Darlene Zschech, David Holmes
© 2004 Hillsong Music Publishing
Recorded on For All You've Done © Hillsong Music Australia

God Is Able
Chapter 11
Ben Fielding, Reuben Morgan, Arrangement by Michael Guy Chislett
© 2010 Hillsong Music Publishing
Recorded on God Is Able© Hillsong Music Australia

God So Loved
Chapter 8
Reuben Morgan
© 2000 Hillsong Music Publishing
Recorded on You Are My World © Hillsong Music Australia

Grace To Grace
Chapters 5, 16
Chris Davenport, Joel Houston
© 2016 Hillsong Music Publishing
Recorded on Let There Be Light © Hillsong Music Australia

Heart Like Heaven
Chapters 11, 14, 15
Matt Crocker, Joel Houston
© 2015 Hillsong Music Publishing
Recorded on Empires © Hillsong Music Australia

Highest
Chapters 10, 15
Reuben Morgan
© 2002 Hillsong Music Publishing
Recorded on Hope © Hillsong Music Australia

His Glory Appears
Chapter 16
Marty Sampson, Darlene Zschech
© 2009 Hillsong Music Publishing & Wondrous Worship (Administered by Music Services o/b/o Llano Music LLC)
All Rights Reserved Used By Permission.
Recorded on Faith + Hope + Love © Hillsong Music Australia

I Adore
Chapter 11
Reuben Morgan
© 2001 Hillsong Music Publishing
Recorded on King Of Majesty © Hillsong Music Australia

In Control
Chapter 16
Ben Fielding, Aodhan King
© 2016 Hillsong Music Publishing
Recorded on Let There Be Light © Hillsong Music Australia

I Surrender
Chapters 11, 13, 14, 15
Matt Crocker
© 2011 Hillsong Music Publishing
Recorded on Cornerstone © Hillsong Music Australia

Jesus Is My Superhero
Chapter 10
Beci Wakerley, David Wakerley
© 2004 Hillsong Music Publishing
Recorded on Hope © Hillsong Music Australia

Jesus The Same
Chapter 10
Raymond Badham
© 2003 Hillsong Music Publishing
Recorded on For All You've Done © Hillsong Music Australia

Jesus What A Beautiful Name
Chapter 12
Tanya Riches
© 1995 Hillsong Music Publishing
Recorded on God Is In The House © Hillsong Music Australia

Just Let Me Say
Chapter 12
Geoff Bullock
© 1993 Geoff Bullock Music
Recorded on People Just Like Us © Hillsong Music Australia

King Of Majesty
Appendix B
Marty Sampson
© 2001 Hillsong Music Publishing
Recorded on King Of Majesty © Hillsong Music Australia

Let Creation Sing
Chapter 10
Reuben Morgan
© 2005 Hillsong Music Publishing
Recorded on God He Reigns © Hillsong Music Australia

Let Us Adore
Chapter 10
Reuben Morgan
© 2005 Hillsong Music Publishing
Recorded on God He Reigns © Hillsong Music Australia

Let There Be Light
Chapters 8, 9, 10, 11, 13, 14, 16
Matthew Crocker, Joel Houston, Michael Guy Chislett, Brooke Ligertwood, Scott Ligertwood, Jonas Myrin
© 2016 Hillsong Music Publishing
Recorded on Let There Be Light © Hillsong Music Australia

Made Me Glad
Chapter 11
Miriam Webster
© 2001 Wonder Down Under Music (admin. by Music Services o/b/o Barton Springs Music, LLC)
All Rights Reserved. Used By Permission.
Recorded on Blessed © Hillsong Music Australia

Magnificent
Chapter 8
Raymond Badham
© 2001 Hillsong Music Publishing
Recorded on Blessed© Hillsong Music Australia

Man Of Sorrows
Chapters 4, 8, 13, 15 and Section 5
Matt Crocker, Brooke Ligertwood
© 2012 Hillsong Music Publishing
Recorded on Glorious Ruins © Hillsong Music Australia

Mighty To Save
Chapters 7, 8, 13, 14, 15 and Section 6
Reuben Morgan, Ben Fielding
© 2006 Hillsong Music Publishing
Recorded on The I Heart Revolution: With Hearts as One © Hillsong Music Australia

Mountain
Chapter 10
Matt Crocker, Joel Houston
© 2012 Hillsong Music Publishing
Recorded on Zion © Hillsong Music Australia

More Than Life
Chapters 11, 13
Reuben Morgan
© 2003 Hillsong Music Publishing
Recorded on More Than Life © Hillsong Music Australia

My Hope
Chapters 7, 8, 14
Darlene Zschech
© 2002 Wondrous Worship (Administered by Music Services o/b/o Llano Music LLC)
All Rights Reserved Used By Permission.
Recorded on Hope © Hillsong Music Australia

My Redeemer Lives
Chapter 13
Reuben Morgan
© 1998 Hillsong Music Publishing
Recorded on By Your Side © Hillsong Music Australia

Need You Here
Chapters 10, 13
Reuben Morgan
© 2001 Hillsong Music Publishing
Recorded on Hope © Hillsong Music Australia

No Other Name
Chapters 4, 8, 9, 11, 13, 14, 15, 16
Jonas Myrin, Joel Houston
© 2014 Hillsong Music Publishing
Recorded on No Other Name © Hillsong Music Australia

Not Today
Chapters 10, 13, 14, 15, 16
Joel Houston, Matt Crocker
© 2017 Hillsong Music Publishing
Recorded on Wonder © Hillsong Music Australia

Oceans
Chapters 8, 9, 11, 13, 14 and Section 4
Matt Crocker, Joel Houston, Salomon Ligthelm
© 2012 Hillsong Music Publishing
Recorded on Zion © Hillsong Music Australia

One Way
Chapters 9, 12, 14
Jonathon Douglass, Joel Houston
© 2003 Hillsong Music Publishing
Recorded on More Than Life © Hillsong Music Australia

Only Wanna Sing
Chapter 8
Aodhan King, Ben Tan, Michael Fatkin
© 2015 Hillsong Music Publishing
Recorded on Youth Revival © Hillsong Music Australia

O Praise The Name (Anástasis)
Chapters 4, 5, 8, 12, 13, 14 and Section 5
Marty Sampson, Benjamin Hastings, Dean Ussher
© 2015 Hillsong Music Publishing
Recorded on Open Heaven / River Wild © Hillsong Music Australia

Open Heaven (River Wild)
Chapters 13, 15, 16
Matt Crocker, Marty Sampson
© 2015 Hillsong Music Publishing
Recorded on Open Heaven / River Wild © Hillsong Music Australia

Passion
Chapters 13, 15, 16
Bede Benjamin-Korporaal, Ben Tan, Laura Toggs, Aodhan King,
© 2015 Hillsong Music Publishing
Recorded on Youth Revival © Hillsong Music Australia

Prince Of Peace
Chapters 8, 11, 13
Joel Houston, Matt Crocker, Dylan Thomas
© 2015 Hillsong Music Publishing
Recorded on Empires © Hillsong Music Australia

Real Love
Chapters 9, 17
Michael Fatkin, Hannah Hobbs, Alex Pappas
© 2015 Hillsong Music Publishing
Recorded on Youth Revival © Hillsong Music Australia

Saviour
Chapter 8
Darlene Zschech
© 2004 Wondrous Worship (Administered by Music Services o/b/o Llano Music LLC)
All Rights Reserved Used By Permission.
Recorded on God He Reigns © Hillsong Music Australia

Scandal Of Grace
Chapters 8, 10
Matt Crocker, Joel Houston
© 2012 Hillsong Music Publishing
Recorded on Zion © Hillsong Music Australia

Shadow Step
Chapter 8
Joel Houston, Michael Guy Chislett
© 2017 Hillsong Music Publishing
Recorded on Wonder © Hillsong Music Australia

Shout To The Lord
Chapter 14 and Section 5
Darlene Zschech
© 1993 Wondrous Worship Music (a div. of Llano Music, LLC)
Recorded on People Just Like Us © Hillsong Music Australia

Sing (Your Love)
Chapters 8, 11, 12
Reuben Morgan
© 2003 Hillsong Music Publishing
Recorded on For All You've Done © Hillsong Music Australia

Sinking Deep
Chapter 6
Joel Davies,   Aodhan King
© 2012 Hillsong Music Publishing
Recorded on Youth Revival © Hillsong Music Australia

Splinters And Stones
Chapter 8, 10
Joel Houston, Michael Guy Chislett
© 2017 Hillsong Music Publishing
Recorded on Wonder © Hillsong Music Australia

Soldier
Chapter 16
Tulele Faletolu, Marty Sampson
© 2003 Hillsong Music Publishing
Recorded on More Than Life © Hillsong Music Australia

So Will I (100 Billion Times)
Chapters 10, 13
Joel Houston, Benjamin Hastings, Michael Fatkin
© 2017 Hillsong Music Publishing
Recorded on Wonder © Hillsong Music Australia

Song Of Freedom
Chapter 15
Marty Sampson
© 2003 Hillsong Music Publishing
Recorded on Song Of Freedom © Hillsong Music Australia

Take All Of Me
Chapter 10
Marty Sampson
© 2003 Hillsong Music Publishing
Recorded on More Than Life © Hillsong Music Australia

Thank You Jesus
Chapter 18
Matt Crocker, Hannah Hobbs
© 2013 Hillsong Music Publishing
Recorded on No Other Name © Hillsong Music Australia

There Is Nothing Like
Chapter 11
Marty Sampson, Jonas Myrin
© 2004 Hillsong Music Publishing
Recorded on Look To You © Hillsong Music Australia

This I Believe (The Creed)
Chapters 5, 12 and Section 2
Matt Crocker, Ben Fielding
© 2014 Hillsong Music Publishing
Recorded on No Other Name © Hillsong Music Australia

Through It All
Appendix B
Reuben Morgan
© 2001 Hillsong Music Publishing
Recorded on Blessed © Hillsong Music Australia

To You Alone
Chapters 8, 12, 14, 15
Reuben Morgan
© 2003 Hillsong Music Publishing
Recorded on For All You've Done © Hillsong Music Australia

Touch The Sky
Chapter 8
Joel Houston, Dylan Thomas, Michael Guy Chislett
© 2015 Hillsong Music Publishing
Recorded on Empires © Hillsong Music Australia

Transfiguration
Chapters 7, 9, 12, 14, 15
Brooke Ligertwood, Scott Ligertwood, Aodhan King, Taya Smith
© 2015 Hillsong Music Publishing
Recorded on Open Heaven / River Wild © Hillsong Music Australia

Wake
Chapter 16
Joel Davies, Hannah Hobbs, Alexander Pappas
© 2013 Hillsong Music Publishing
Recorded on We Are Young And Free © Hillsong Music Australia

Water To Wine
Chapters 12, 14
Joel Houston
© 2017 Hillsong Music Publishing
Recorded on Wonder © Hillsong Music Australia

What A Beautiful Name
Chapters 8, 11, 12, 13, 14 and Section 3
Ben Fielding, Brooke Ligertwood
© 2016 Hillsong Music Publishing
Recorded on Let There Be Light © Hillsong Music Australia

What The Lord Has Done
Chapter 8
Reuben Morgan
© 1999 Hillsong Music Publishing
Recorded on By Your Side © Hillsong Music Australia

With All I Am
Chapters 8, 11, 13
Reuben Morgan
© 2003 Hillsong Music Publishing
Recorded on For All You've Done © Hillsong Music Australia

Worthy Is The Lamb
Chapters 8, 10, 14
Darlene Zschech
© 2000 Wondrous Worship (Administered by Music Services o/b/o Llano Music LLC)
All Rights Reserved. Used By Permission.
Recorded on You Are My World © Hillsong Music Australia

You Are
Appendix B
Darlene Zschech
© 2003 Wondrous Worship (Administered by Music Services o/b/o Llano Music LLC)
All Rights Reserved Used By Permission.
Recorded on Hope © Hillsong Music Australia

You Are Worthy
Chapters 8, 11, 14
Darlene Zschech
© 2003 Wondrous Worship (Administered by Music Services o/b/o Llano Music LLC)
All Rights Reserved Used By Permission.
Recorded on For All You've Done © Hillsong Music Australia

Yours Is The Kingdom
Chapter 11
Joel Houston
© 2005 Hillsong Music Publishing
Recorded on God He Reigns © Hillsong Music Australia

Your Word
Chapters 10, 13, 14, 16
Chris Davenport
© 2016 Hillsong Music Publishing
Recorded on Let There Be Light © Hillsong Music Australia

Other Songs

Amazing Grace
Chapter 8, 12
John Newton
Traditional

America
Chapter 16
Bernstein/Sondheim

Blessed Be Your Name
Appendix B (quoted)
Beth and Matt Redman
© 2002 Thankyou Music (Admin. by Crossroad Distributors Pty. Ltd.)

Bring Him Home
Chapter 14
Boublil/Schonberg,

Close Every Door
Chapter 16
Lloyd Webber/Rice

Everything's Alright
Chapter 16
Lloyd Webber/Rice

Fly Me To The Moon
Chapter 15
Bart Howard

Go Down Moses
Chapter 15
Unknown

Hark The Herald Angels Sing
Chapters 7, 12 (quoted)
Charles Wesley, Felix Mendelssohn
Traditional

Habanera
Chapter 14
Georges Bizet

In The Whisper Of A Moment
Chapter 2 (quoted)

Jenny Keating

Joshua Fought The Battle Of Jericho
Chapter 15
Jay Roberts

Majesty
Chapter 14
Stu Garrard, Martin Smith

My Favourite Things
Chapter 16
Rodgers/Hammerstein

No More
Chapter 12
Stephen Sondheim

Over The Rainbow
Chapter 14
Harburg/Arlen

People
Chapter 14
Styne/Merrill

Phantom of the Opera
Chapter 14
Lloyd Webber/Hart

Silent Night
Chapter 12, 15
Joseph Mohr, Franz Xaver Gruber

Summertime
Chapter 14
George Gershwin

Temple Song
Chapter 16
Lloyd Webber/Rice

The First Nowell
Chapter 8
Unknown

There's a Place For Us
Chapter 14
Bernstein/Sondheim

Three Blind Mice
Chapter 15
Unknown

When I Survey The Wondrous Cross
Chapter 11, 12 (quoted)
Isaac Watts
Traditional

While Shepherds Watched Their Flocks By Night
Chapter 8
Este's Psalmes

Yesterday
Chapter 12, 14
Lennon/McCartney

You'll Never Walk Alone
Chapter 12
Rodgers/Hammerstein

BOOK REFERENCES

Bobbie Houston *Heaven is in this House* Maximised Leadership Inc. Australia 2001
(Introductory thoughts)

Enhanced Strong's Lexicon Oak Harbor, WA: Logos Research Systems, Inc. 1995
Chapter 1

Leonard Bernstein *The Joy of Music* Panther Books USA 1969
Chapter 1

C.S.Lewis *Reflections on the Psalms (Selected Books)* Harper Collins UK 1999
Chapter 2

Madeleine L'Engle *Walking on Water* Waterbrook Press USA 1972
Chapter 3

Daniel Barenboim and Edward Said *Parallels and Paradoxes* Bloomsbury Publishing PLC UK 2002
Chapter 6, 14, 15

Martin Luther quoted in Richard Viladesau *Theology and the Arts* Paulist Press USA 2000
Chapter 7, Section 5

Ross Clifford & Philip Johnson *The Cross is not enough* USA Baker Books 2012
Chapter 7

Abraham Heschel *The Prophets* Perennial Classics New York USA 2001
Chapter 10

Walter Breuggemann *The Message of the Psalms* Augsburg, Minneapolis USA 1984
Appendix A

Tremper Longman III *How to Read the Psalms* IVP UK 1988
Appendix B

ACKNOWLEDGEMENTS

It is almost impossible to thank everyone who has contributed to the writing of this book but I want to thank some who have had a particular part to play.

Thank you firstly to my husband Robert, who has always encouraged me to write. You are my best friend and most honest critic and, have influenced my life so deeply. Thank you for writing the wonderful chapter on a theology of worship and for the journey we have been on as we have checked the lyrics of countless songs.

Thank you also to my three children, two sons in law and daughter in law and seven grandchildren who have enriched my life so much and who have been great cheer leaders along the way. Thank you to my parents who instilled in me a love for words and music.

Thankyou Darlene, dear friend, for your encouragement to write the book in the first place. Thank you Cassandra and so many others for encouraging me to work on this new edition of the book. Thank you Joel for your beautiful and gracious foreword to this new edition.

Thank you Daryl-Anne, Laura, Josh, Tim, Jay and others for taking my manuscript and turning it into a book. Thank you Steve for your great chapter on the business of song writing and for all your other help. Thank you to so many others including Craig, Peter and Sydney for your help with matters musical and Annie who did all the original interviews.

Thank you all the songwriters at Hillsong Church who contributed your comments and wrote such wonderful songs that have become my illustrations.

Thank you all my song writing students who taught me so much about song writing and its joys and pitfalls.

Thank you Brian and Bobbie, my senior pastors, for backing this book and allowing it to be produced as a Hillsong resource. Thank you for being the sort of leaders who inspire us to attempt such things.

Thank you above all to my Lord and Saviour Jesus Christ who I love more with every passing year. You are worthy of all the praise in every song that we could ever write and so much more.

(Footnotes)

1   Joel Houston- *'Joel Houston talks ZION'* https://hillsong.com/collected/blog/2013/02/joel-houston-talks-zion/#.WVSjuIiGOM8   7/2/2013 Used by permission

2   Joel Houston – *'Broken Vessels Song Story'* https://hillsong.com/collected/blog/2014/07/broken-vessels-song-story/#.WVSWSIiGOM8   14/7/2014 Used by permission

3   Reuben Morgan –*'When talent is not enough'* https://hillsong.com/collected/blog/2015/11/when-talent-is-not-enough/#.WVSYaIiGOM8 23/11/2015 Used by permission

4   Joel Houston – *'Joel Houston talks ZION.* https://hillsong.com/collected/blog/2013/02/joel-houston-talks-zion/#.WVSjuIiGOM8   27/2/2013 Used by permission

5   Joel Houston – *'The White album'* https://hillsong.com/collected/blog/2014/03/the-white-album-a-remix-project/#.WVSb64iGOM8 1/3/2014 Used by permission

6   Adapted Marty Sampson - *'Song Story: O Praise The Name (Anástasis)'* 6/10/2015 Used by permission
https://hillsong.com/collected/blog/2015/10/song-story-o-praise-the-name-anastasis/#.WVSdO4iGOM8

7   Matt Crocker – *'The Fingerprint of a Song'* https://hillsong.com/collected/blog/2012/07/the-fingerprint-of-a-song/#.WVSZ74iGOM8   9/7/2012 Used by permission

8   Ben Fielding - '3 Questions a song writer should as before writing another song'. https://hillsong.com/collected/blog/2016/06/3-questions-a-song-writer-should-ask-before-writing-another-song/#.WVSfWIiGOM8 14/6/16 Used by permission.

9   Ben Fielding – 'Anchor [Song Story]' https://hillsong.com/collected/blog/2013/07/anchor-song-story/#.WVSgmoiGOM8 16/7/2013 Used by permission

10 Ben Fielding – '5 things to have in mind when writing a congregational song' https://hillsong.com/collected/blog/2015/03/5-things-to-have-in-mind-when-writing-a-congregational-song/#.WVShJoiGOM8 5/3/2015 Used by permission.

11 Marty Sampson -'Open Heaven (River Wild) Song Story' 29/11/2015 Used by permission. https://hillsong.com/collected/blog/2015/11/open-heaven-river-wild-song-story/#.WVSioIiGOM8

12 Hannah Hobbs - 'Thank You Jesus Song Story' https://hillsong.com/collected/blog/2014/07/thank-you-jesus-song-story/#.WVSjHYiGOM8 23/7/2014 Used by permission.

Lightning Source UK Ltd.
Milton Keynes UK
UKHW042210061218
333575UK00002B/94/P